THE UNMANIFEST SELF

THE UNMANIFEST SELF

Transcending the Limits of Ordinary Consciousness

by
Ligia Dantes

Published by

Aslan Publishing
310 Blue Ridge Drive
Boulder Creek, CA 95006
(408) 338-7504

Dantes, Ligia, 1929-
    The unmanifest self: transcending the limits of ordinary
consciousness / by Ligia Dantes. — 1st ed.
        p. cm.
    Includes bibliographical references.
    ISBN 0-944031-17-X : $14.95. — ISBN 0-944031-16-1 (pbk.) : $9.95
    1. Self. 2. Individualism—Psychological aspects.
3. Individualism—Social aspects. I. Title.
BF697.D32   1990
155.2—dc20

Book design by Philip Gill
Cover design by Brenda Plowman
Cover photo copyright, The Image Bank
Printed in USA
First Edition

10 9 8 7 6 5 4 3 2 1

This book is dedicated to

Edward, Adela and Elisa,
my children and my great teachers in humanness;
to

Armando Riesco Puyol,
for his unwavering dedication to inquiry,
and for his loving, unconditional generosity;
and to

Humanity,
the manifestation of universal essence.

ACKNOWLEDGEMENTS

This book is based mainly on the experience of life itself, the life of human beings on the planet, and only partly on the knowledge of psychology and other sciences. I am infinitely grateful to my family, friends, humanity at large and life in the universe. These are, as it were, the bibliography of this book. I wish to specifically acknowledge some of the many people who have contributed to my life and therefore to the rendition of this book.

I am grateful to:

Joanne Crandall, for her infinite loving energy and countless hours of work;

Virginia Gordon, our pillar of love and support, who quietly and humbly gives of herself unconditionally;

Philip Gill, for his unceasing dedication to inquiry, and his loving cooperation;

Dr. Stuart Over, for his love, humor, deep understanding, and unconditional giving;

Robert Powell, for giving so freely of his time to write the foreword, as well as being my patient writing mentor; and to his wife, *Gina Powell,* for her understanding and loving support of my work.

I am especially indebted to my mother, *Carmen Vera,* for her kindness and wisdom; my father, *Juan Bloise,* my sister, *Alba Moasser*, and my daughter-in-law, *Kristy Andrews*, for their tenacity of character; *Ellis Andrews* for introducing me to psychology; and *Dr. Glenn Mahan* for introducing me to Zen and other spiritual philosophies.

I am grateful to *Dr. William Sullivan* for pointing to the existential nature of humans, excluded from the process of psychoanalysis; and to *Werner Erhard* for giving me the space to be free and showing me the meaning of unconditional love.

I have special gratitude for *Koban Chino Roshi* for illuminating the path through the darkness of conditioning and for pointing to truth. His clarity and gentle spirit have been a total inspiration in my work.

Special thanks to *Dr. Gloria Russell-Collins*, a beautiful being, whose deep understanding of human nature illuminates her work as a psychologist; to *Mahli Caron*, who from the beginning has contributed lovingly and unconditionally, for her fortitude in inquiry; to *Setti Mirus*, a beautiful, gentle energy and to her husband, *Ferdinand*, for their continuous love and support.

To my old friends *Enrico* and *Nadia Natali*, *Idee Levitan*, *Leita Alenskis*, *Annette Levey*, *Renee Ketcham*, *Fred Colcer*, *Jean-Luc Gaudremeau*, *Gordon Ellis*, *Bill Smythe*, *Cynthia Velez*, *Loren Spence*, *Jane Riskin*, *Ann Dobroth*, *Lynne Thurston*, and *Phil Johnson* many thanks for their loving support.

To all my friends in Puerto Rico who have been contributing to my work there.

I'd like to acknowledge *Peter Garrett* and *Lesley Wilson* for their deep understanding of this book and for encouragement and assistance in the publication process. I am especially grateful to *Brenda Plowman* and *Dawson Church* for their clarity, loving support, and faith in this book.

Finally, a note of thanks to *Dr. David Bohm* and to the late *Krishnamurti*, guiding lights for many people in the world in the process of self-inquiry.

CONTENTS

ABOUT THE AUTHOR
by Philip Gill

I first heard Ligia Dantes speak in a small living room in Ojai, California. Diminutive and soft-spoken, she seemed very ordinary in most respects, yet there was something decidedly unordinary about the way she related to me and the dozen or so other people present. There was an alertness, a sensitivity, and a deep caring toward every single person in the room—as if she had come to hear us rather than the other way around. As I came to know more about Ligia, I discovered that this impression was more significant than I at first realized.

Even as a young girl growing up in Uruguay, she had always exhibited an unusual sensitivity and curiosity. A deep interest in others and a strong desire to understand life were part of her nature. Although she grew up normally, she had experiences of a spiritual nature as a child, which she didn't understand until years later. Because of her youth, little importance was attached to those experiences at the time. Even now, with much deeper understanding, she still attaches little significance to such occurrences. Personal experiences are important to Ligia only insofar as they relate to life as a whole. Her focus is always toward others, toward what is needed in humanity.

After she came to the United States at the age of eighteen, she settled in California, married and raised three children. Though her intense curiosity never left her, it was not until her children matured that she began to pursue her interests with a fervor. She threw herself into acquiring an education in psychology with the goal of practicing as a psychoanalyst—even completing five years of analysis herself, which was then required for certification. But after nearly eight years of education and training she had an experience that radically shifted her perception of society and the direction of her life. She saw a society desperately in need of self-understanding; she experienced the violence in humanity and the urgent need for people to wake up. Suddenly a career as a psychoanalyst, though lucrative, seemed too limited and too self-serving. She dropped her career goals and began a kind of firsthand investigation and inquiry into life, which continues to this day. It was the beginning of a process that has brought her to a life completely devoted to the service of others. And it is this process that she shares in this book and in everything she does.

Ligia realized that the value of a questioning mind and service to others is not something you teach or learn about; it is something you live. What is important is the *action*—a commitment to investigate, look, and experience life first-hand. Such a complete kind of inquiry brings about a totally different kind of living in and of itself. There's no knowledge that must be acquired. It was this realization that moved her to create the Self-Studies Foundation. She felt the need to serve any individual who had the desire to inquire more deeply into life.

Many people come to Self-Studies dialogues and seminars top-heavy with years of accumulated knowledge about spiritual subjects. They come to find out what Ligia is teaching. Actually, she doesn't have a teaching. Although her own training has included disciplines from est to Zen and exposure to many others, she neither endorses nor rejects any of them. She has an astonishing ability to access what is precisely appropriate for an individual at a particular moment. Always with incredible caring and love, Ligia encourages people to comprehend the difference between an intellectual understanding and the reality of living action. She gently urges people toward an objective self-observation without self-criticism, judgment, or evaluation.

Volunteers for Self-Studies and people who work with Ligia on a regular basis find their lives changing in ways they never would have predicted. Observing themselves in everyday situations, they begin to realize to what an alarming extent their behavior is automatic and unconscious. This observation process is uncommonly subtle and paradoxical. The more we look inward to understand our own behavior, the more we are drawn outward to serve others; the more we allow uncomfortable and perturbing feelings without trying to escape from them, the more harmonious our lives become. I have never worked with a group of people who were more mature and worked together with less friction than the people involved in the Self-Studies Foundation. This objective observation process begins to bring about the kind of alertness, sensitivity, and caring that I observed in Ligia the first day I met her. Also, there seems to be a resonance effect of being around someone like Ligia who lives exactly as she speaks. She creates an energy like an ocean swell, gentle and flowing, but with mass, power, and movement. Always the invitation is extended to break out of the confines of your intellect and live that energy.

There really is no substitute for a person to person experience with someone like Ligia. Just the same, many people asked Ligia to write this book. She was quite hesitant to add yet one more contribution to the heaving sea of intellectual literature on transformational topics. But I think she has produced an excellent book with a unique approach. The style of reader-author interaction is surprisingly close to the way she works in person. If readers can just resist their habitual reading patterns and give themselves over to the interactive process of this book, they will have an opportunity to experience a new kind of awareness.

The world desperately needs human beings like Ligia Dantes—individuals of clarity, compassion, and uncompromising integrity, with a deep comprehension of the way human beings function. We need genuine, whole, committed people who live ordinary lives, who teach by speaking the truth and by living what they speak. There is not now, nor will there ever be, any credential or accrediting organization that can assure us that a teacher has these qualities. But anyone who is a little sensitive can know when they've found such a person. Lucky is the individual with an inquiring mind who has found someone like Ligia Dantes.

FOREWORD
by Robert Powell

The most urgent need for us as humans is to become
more conscious of our at present largely unconscious
mode of functioning. We are little more than the sum total
of our conditioning, of which we are not even faintly
aware. So the problem is: Who is going to awaken us from
this slumberlike condition?

Throughout time, there have been teachers who have
aimed at bringing a greater degree of awareness to humanity, but in too many cases their appeals have fallen on deaf
ears, their teachings being either too esoteric, directed at a
select few, or beyond the capacity for understanding of the
majority of people. So there exists a great need for teachers
and books that are geared for those who do not want to get
involved with any particular school of thought or "ism "
that is likely to be yet another form of conditioning. This
means, for example, that a writer, instead of dealing with
the subject of consciousness, must coax readers to deal
with it instead, so that they may make their own discoveries. In all this, the teacher by merely asking the pertinent

questions, serves purely as catalyst. This prevents students from getting rid of their existing conditioning only to replace it with fresh conditioning from their latest teacher. I know of very few works that follow this kind of approach. But now Ligia Dantes has written a guidebook that I foresee will serve the purpose admirably. She very gently and ably takes the reader on a journey of self-exploration, stopping at each step of the way to let the greater awareness flood in at its own pace and yet never filling these moments of silent observation with any concepts of her own.

Ligia is well qualified to write such a work. For years, she has been giving lectures and seminars to thousands of people in many parts of the world. Originally a psychotherapist, she is one of the few who recognized the limits of that calling in dealing with the human psyche on its most fundamental level. I feel privileged to have known Ligia for a number of years and to have had the pleasure of seeing her in action at her meetings. On such occasions, I had to admire her capability of putting even the most disturbed souls at ease just by the magic of her silent presence.

I warmly recommend her book to all those who are thoroughly dissatisfied with the everyday travails of their existence and yearn for a different way of life—that spiritual dimension in which their functioning is no longer rooted in concept but is the spontaneous expression from moment to moment of the liberating insights of authentic self-inquiry. Ligia gives them a place to start.

PREFACE
by Stuart Over, M.D.

The Unmanifest Self is not an ordinary self-help book, just as the author, Ligia Dantes, is not an ordinary New Age writer. Ligia has a unique ability to serve as a reflection or mirror of an individual's inner wisdom and to facilitate that person's utilization of that wisdom in understanding his or her own nature.

Several years ago, Ligia established the Self-Studies Foundation, a non profit, educational institution with the purpose of serving humanity through inquiry and study of the functioning of the individual as a holistic part of humanity. She devotes her entire time and energy to this end, and *The Unmanifest Self* is based on her insights and on the vital daily process the volunteers and participants experience in their interactions with her.

The principles and practices set forth in the book are a reflection of the practical daily relationships between Ligia and her friends in the Foundation. These practices have been proved effective by the way in which they have affected the lives of those around her. Ligia is firm in her denial that she is a "teacher," or that she has "students." Her friends honor this denial, although they are equally firm in their conviction that they have learned a great deal from her as a mentor and a loyal, wise friend.

In the actual practice of the group and individual dialogues, the meditations and retreats that expose the participants to Ligia's wisdom and loving kindness, the emphasis is not on changing the individual's thinking, but on facilitating him or her to become aware of the enormous burden of conditioning that accumulates in each of us during our childhood and years of education and in fact throughout our entire lives. Awareness of how this conditioning affects our thoughts, emotions and actions helps us to direct our thoughts and energy in a more loving and compassionate manner.

One of Ligia's fundamental principles is that each of us is responsible not only for our own actions but also for those of all humanity, of which we are an integral part. This was manifested to me in a dramatic fashion on a trip I made to China last year. I was in Shanghai on the day the Chinese celebrated the anniversary of the communist revolution. The streets around the Peace Hotel where we were staying were filled with a solid mass of Chinese people. They stretched as far as one could see, moving slowly past the hotel. I stood on the steps and had actual physical contact with the children and parents streaming by. I felt a bonding with these people, a feeling of love and compassion and kinship that has changed my perception of life. I was indeed joined with and a part of humanity during those moments.

This insight and many more of my own and those of other people associated with Ligia have made significant changes in our way of living. I feel certain that those who are sincerely interested in inquiry and self discovery, who read and act upon Ligia's book, will experience insights that will help them to live a more loving and compassionate life and thus to be of service to humanity.

You:
A Significant Event in the Universe

You and I are about to embark on a process of discovery through questioning everything from the most obvious to the most hidden in our consciousness. I feel privileged to enter into this relationship with you. Together we will open the doors imprisoning humanity's soul.

In the first part of the book we will observe the predicament of humanity at large. The emphasis is on the generally ignoble situation on our planet. Consideration of these problems is perturbing and may at first give an impression of negativity in our approach. However, it is my intention to attend to what is most needed. It is necessary to confront that which we might be unconsciously avoiding because it is unpleasant.

We also want to acknowledge, however, the wonderful achievements in science and medicine; the efficient and altruistic behavior of many not-so-well-known politicians, consumer advocates, and business and community leaders who use their positions to bring about awareness of the

need for peace and concern about ecology; religious leaders who speak for harmony and compassion all over the
world and who make an outstanding contribution to the
poor; and finally, the thousands of lesser known individuals of all nations who are working fervently to feed the
poor, shelter the homeless, care for the sick, and bring
peace to humankind.

It is not my intention to ignore the greatness of human
beings at large. It is because of the basic love-nature of
humanity that we want to explore deeply the impediments
hindering the total expression of human compassion. This
compassion is in all of us equally, but we are not living this
loving nature in daily life on the planet. It is within the
context of human compassion that I am writing this book.

Trusting Your Direct Experience

Human beings are entrapped in a mire of conditioning.
Unaware of this fact, we behave in a way that is taking us
to the brink of extinction. This dangerous trap of conditioned habitual behavior has inadvertently been caused by
the accumulation of our scientific, technological, and religious knowledge. Even so, you and I can responsibly utilize part of this conditioned knowledge to bring about a
different consciousness in our world. In our case, we will
use written language, *without a specific authority to guide us.*

Chapters Two through Four in particular are devoted
to a deep and serious global observation of humanity's
predicament and, as such, may seem difficult. Therefore
you may want to put the book down from time to time to
ponder what you have read. In later chapters we will be
observing the personal, or individual, functioning. The
subtitles mark a series of natural and continuing flare-ups
of the thought process.

This book is written in a casual style as if you and I
were personally talking, probing, questioning. It is a sort of

free-flowing conversation, with the typical meandering of our minds. I propose to carry on this imaginary dialogue in a rather impersonal manner, so we can see ourselves directly, in an all-encompassing view.

You will notice that throughout this book you and I will depend mostly on ourselves for the direct experience of facts, rather than on information from scientists, religious leaders, or other authors. We do not need to justify our inquiry or quote the great works of others to prove our points or authenticate our discoveries. We will deepen our exploration in an atmosphere of "not knowing." By "not knowing," I mean we trust our own insights. In this manner you and I will be trusting a wisdom beyond our conscious knowledge, the wisdom that illuminated the sages.

To reach the depth of the soul, that which is unmanifest, we have to travel through uncomfortable or perturbing truths about our present human condition. We need to be responsible, and we need the courage to withstand the persistent desire for comfort. The tendency to avoid pain and crave pleasure is characteristic of our consciousness. To be able to transcend this consciousness, to be accessible to that which is beyond it, we need the strength of steel and the flexibility of the willow. On the other hand, we need a stillness to be with all emotions, without trying to change them, yet not be attached to them. We also need to be totally open to great joy without attachment.

When you and I are in the experience of "being humanity" rather than separate beings, and when our dialogue is devoid of my personal inner experiences as an author, then your own experience becomes the most important event. It is my intent that you be, at the moment of reading, a significant phenomenon in the universe. At that moment, the magic of "you being humanity itself" is an event in the universal energy, the Unmanifest, as powerful and brilliant as a nova in celestial space.

While celebrating a young friend's birthday, I was inspired to write this short poem:

> In honor of your
> being
> I wanted to bring
> to you the most
> beautiful thing in
> the world.
> For that, I would
> have to bring
> YOU to yourself.
> Unable to do this,
> I brought you this
> rose, which is the
> same.

I hope this book can represent that rose I would personally bring to you in honor of your being!

Now let us begin our journey.

The Butterfly:
The Urgency of Humanity's Metamorphosis

Humankind cannot survive on this planet without a major shift in our way of thinking and functioning. Our children and all the children after them deserve an abundant, naturally beautiful planet and a way of living that is harmonious. We need a significant mass of human beings to dedicate their energy and attend to the global necessities. We are responsible for bringing about awareness in a mostly somnolent humanity. To become aware ourselves and to share with others in this awareness is like lighting a fuse to bring about an explosion of light into consciousness.

Truly aware living is transformation. What is truly needed for humanity's survival is a radical change, a transformation, a transubstantiation, if you will.

Transformation is a process of deep change in the functioning of the organism's structure. It is a psychophysiological revolution, analogous to the change of the chrysalis into the butterfly, the difference being that the outer form of the human organism remains the same. But the cells and the chemistry of the body are deeply affected, and this is reflected in the person's behavior.

Embracing Discomfort

Influenced by idealistic philosophies, some people have fallen into a belief that transformation comes like lightning and suddenly everything is wonderful. They have the idea that they are enlightened and there are no more real problems in their way.

Human transformation is a natural process, a movement in the manifest energy we call *homo sapiens*. We may feel the deep transforming changes as extremely powerful, mind-boggling, ego-annihilating, and physically discomforting. On the other hand, within this process there may be periods of radiant insight, a sense of total well-being, quiet mind, or ecstasy. It is the nature of the human organism to feel, sense, experience dualistic forces within. To be fully aware, one must be willing to be totally perturbed as well as to be in rapture.

To feel ourselves whole, complete, undivided, is to experience our sacredness.

Your job is to become deeply, totally aware; aware with your *whole being* of this need for change at the root of your functioning as humanity. You are responsible for the whole. You, and you alone, are the awareness of the consciousness of humankind.

> ✤ *A shift in your consciousness is a shift in human consciousness. Are you willing to experience and assume this responsibility?*

This book aims to create deep understanding of the

need for total change in humanity. It does not aim to transform anyone. The process of transformation is in nature itself, in the universe, in the energy that is eternal.

The human species is part of this energy. We are an aggregate of atoms, a specific arrangement of molecules, creating a particular movement in the ever-changing and transforming energy of the whole. Thus our potential for transformation lies *within our own being*.

> ❦ *If you and I could have a personal dialogue, we would do together the kind of inquiry proposed in this book. As I write these pages I feel a closeness and a deep caring for you, a human being in a process of discovery. I go over these things with hundreds of people, and each time I discover with them anew.*

The challenge to us is to experience ourselves as *humanity* rather than simply as individuals. This book has been written to present an opportunity to meet this challenge. The key passages are indented and in italics to urge readers to "look" without the use of knowledge, without letting the words of the book influence their thinking. It is my intention that all the words—the symbols and ideas—in this book serve as stimuli to the reader's own inquiries and discoveries. My observations throughout the book are intended as a form of self-confrontation rather than a psychological treatise.

The Cocoon of Self-Involvement

While individuals have been cognizant of the potential for transformation—at least a few have—transformation has not occurred in humanity as a whole, despite all the teachings and all the philosophical and religious books written on the subject. Instead, these have become part of the accumulated knowledge passed on through generations in the form of beliefs. The present popular interest in the transformation of consciousness is mostly a fad, based on the belief that individuals can transform themselves. Magazines aimed at the New Age market are filled with ads promising self-transformation. One advertisement reads, "Transform your consciousness through subliminal tapes." Another says, "These tapes lead the listener to spiritual awareness." Thousands of teachers are using the idea of transformation to design meditations, courses, and workshops that claim to transform individuals. The increasing popularity of these endeavors seems to parallel enthusiasms of the past—such as psychoanalysis, transactional analysis, Gestalt therapy—now no longer in popular demand. Encounter groups such as those made popular at Synanon, a drug rehabilitation center in California, are rare these days. Psychoanalysis, a pastime of the rich at one time, is rarely the topic of conversation anymore.

Egotistically believing in self-transformation, people have been trying for hundreds of years to achieve a radical change, developing different techniques and rituals for this purpose. For many seekers of transformation, the New Age of spirituality has brought renewals or composites of the old practices, giving the impression of "new" ways to transform oneself. Transcendental Meditation, introduced by Maharishi Mahesh Yogi of India, has become very popular in the last twenty years, and has moved into the psychological research arena. A large university has been established in Iowa by followers of Transcendental Meditation.

Even modern technology has been engaged in attempts to gain such results. In 1987, a psychologist in Georgia was designing a transformational technique with the use of video. Advertisements in New Age journals promising better meditations, altered states of consciousness, and high spiritual development with the use of "brain machines" are plentiful. One ad claims to produce the effects of ten years of meditation in ten minutes!

If humankind could achieve transformation through knowledge and technology, we would by now be living at peace on the planet. Through intelligence, we would have devised a daily existence in which love is the mainspring of our actions. Instead, we have a general way of living in which acquisitiveness, competition, rituals, pleasure-seeking, fear, and territorialism are the preponderant manifestations.

> ❦ *These words are not directed at you personally, nor are they aimed at any particular group. You and I are looking at that which is not working in humanity.*

The newspapers are filled with horrible stories of crime, especially in large cities such as Los Angeles, Chicago, and New York. The competition is fierce among business tycoons as well as small business owners. The intensity of competition in sports, bringing about violence among fans, has not lessened as we have become more "civilized." In Argentina and England eruptions of violence during soccer games have had tragic results: people have been injured, maimed, and even killed in large melees. News stories about good Samaritans, cooperation in business, and love for one another are heavily outweighed by those about gang wars and children born with AIDS or drug addictions. Love, true compassion, seems to be reserved for the few, instead of being the all-encompassing attitude so needed in the masses.

The Interconnected Human System

We human beings do not carry a self-image encompassing the whole of humanity. We do not see ourselves as the world. The popular song title, "We Are the World," is only a lyrical metaphor that evokes emotional reactions. But the reality, the *fact*, is that we live individualistic lives. We are programmed to live a self-centered existence, whether this centeredness means caring for *my* body, *my* family, *my* school, *my* political views, *my* religion, or *my* nation.

This egocentric way of living is more than the particular life-style of an individual; it enfolds the personal beliefs and survival needs of the collective, based on generations of cultural conditioning. The particular religious, political, or governmental institutions that prevail are part of, and reflect, the "me." This "me" is the object of protection from other "me's," building the religious, racial, and nationalistic fences that engender wars.

✿ *Please look objectively, without pointing fingers at others or blaming yourself.*

Ways of thinking inherited from previous generations deeply affect the individual at the somatic, or cellular, level. Historically the adaptation to a different climate brought about new ways of thinking and consequently a new style of living.

Today our human physique differs from that of our ancestors. For instance, the texture of our skin has become more delicate, less resistant. We have used our intelligence to develop ways of living that protect our skin, through architecture and mechanization. Societal conduct has greatly influenced our somatic (physical) way of functioning.

Inversely, soma (the body) has been, from the very beginning of man's existence, a primary determinant in the formation of the culture. Races developed ways of living in different parts of the world that were appropriate to their physical structure and basic functioning. Human vulnerability in infancy may also be one of many conditioning factors involved in our survival, subsequently influencing behavioral patterns.

Abundant research attests to the behavioral problems developed in children when they are not cared for properly in infancy. We all need close, affectionate relationships with other human beings from birth. One particular case study suggests that depressed behavior in children from one to five years old correlates directly with their upbringing. The children examined were raised in an orphanage, where they were ignored most of the time. Even though they were well fed and cared for physically, they developed very despondent, moody, and uninterested attitudes; some of them became extremely neurotic. Even in infant monkeys, the need for closeness or affection has been proved. When deprived of their mothers, the babies have great difficulty in relating to other monkeys.

Ways of thinking also influence our diet, affecting our body structure and behavior. In our culture, we have developed a taste for certain foods such as sugar, chocolate, and fast foods; we have used our intellect to create a cuisine that eventually changes the organism, affecting our behavior. Hyperactivity in children, for example, is associated with the intake of simple sugars. We all know how our bodies react to mental stimuli such as fear or frustration: our bodies become ill (as with ulcers) or diseased after prolonged periods of such emotions. Conversely, we may be mentally affected—perhaps becoming despondent—when confronted with a serious virus or disease. Sexual stimulation brings about an ecstatic mental state.

The body-mind, or psyche-soma, is not two separate entities, as early twentieth century medicine thought. The human being is one *process*. Being self-conscious, we are now aware of these two facets of our organism and their reciprocity. Human beings exist within larger reciprocal processes; we exist in relationship within larger contexts. We interact with, affect, and are affected, directly or indirectly, by all existence. Our immediate context is the earth. We exist on a planet; the larger context is the universe, which we can only partially perceive. The following diagram elucidates the universal process.

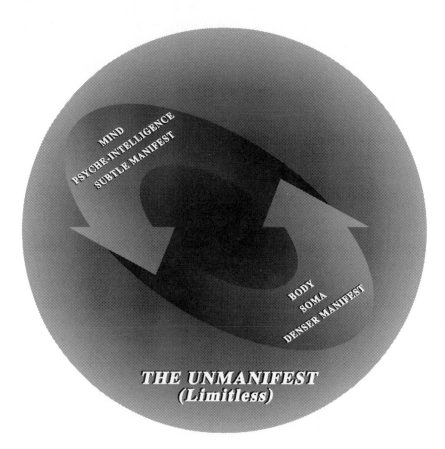

MIND
PSYCHE-INTELLIGENCE
SUBTLE MANIFEST

BODY
SOMA
DENSER MANIFEST

**THE UNMANIFEST
(Limitless)**

The center of the diagram illustrates the reciprocity of influence of the two aspects of the human organism. Both arrows in the diagram contain the word "manifest," because everything is manifest in either dense or subtle form. The circle surrounding the two arrows represents the Unmanifest (the context where creation occurs), that which is totally imperceptible to us—that which is called by gurus and religious leaders God, Spirit, or Universal Mind.

The denser and subtle manifest levels are not units separate from the Unmanifest; they are in a constant cycle of originating and returning (organizing and disorganizing) into the unknown—the Unmanifest. To understand what the Unmanifest Self actually is, we must paradoxically *discover self as both imperceptible unmanifest and subtle-dense manifest at the same time.*

The point here is that the mental and physical are two distinct aspects of human beings—one subtle, the other dense—these being endogenous in nature itself. In this book the mind is considered the subtle function enfolded in the organism (soma), capable of carrying symbols, images, and meaning. Human relationships are based on this mind function. We communicate, interact, and influence one another by thoughts and ideas expressed through words and actions.

The Dictatorship of Knowledge

Modern scientists study individuals based on personal experiences, family and societal background. Consequently, psychology and sociology have been made the undisputed authority for understanding ourselves.

Sigmund Freud's theories have been a basis for understanding our minds for decades. We have looked at ourselves according to his descriptions of id, ego, and superego. We explained and understood ourselves as unconscious, subconscious, and conscious beings. These ways of thinking still reverberate in much of the psychological literature. When Carl Jung postulated his theories, we began to believe in the collective unconscious. With Fritz Perls we explained ourselves as possessing child, parent, and adult personalities within.

    ✿ *But is this the way you really are? Is this not a limited way to see yourself?*

Have you read these kinds of books? Have they influenced the way you see or explain yourself? Perhaps they have been a great help to you. Look at what is factual for you.

Thousands and thousands of people today are asking themselves, "Who am I? Which teacher should I believe?" A lady visited me in 1986 inquiring about her true nature. She wanted knowledge. She had read hundreds of books, gone through Freudian, Jungian, and Gestalt therapies and practiced Transcendental Meditation. She found herself in a quandary. She could *explain* why she felt and acted the way she did. She could *understand* her background and the people in it. Furthermore, she felt she had changed through the years, become mellower, and she was getting along fairly well with people. Still, she remained an enigma to herself. She was forty-two years old and she still did not know, after all her acquired knowledge, what "life was all about." What was her purpose in life? What was unconditional love? She had learned all about it, yet she did not feel that within herself she truly loved.

Together we began by looking at our conditioning and the need for authority. After she recognized her own hankering for security, as well as her dependency on and belief in an authority, she was faced with the need to take responsibility for her own way of living. At the end of her visit she was relieved; she said, "For the first time I feel at home within myself."

You Are Your Own Authority

This book proposes that you be your own authority, the only one discerning, observing, and holistically viewing, through your own wisdom, what is meant by such terms as "the psychosomatic nature of human beings," "spirituality," "mind," and so on. The suggestion is to use this book as a stimulus for your own experiencing rather than as a source of information and authority.

> ✿ *Please look at the statements in the*
> *following paragraph and see if you feel*
> *they are true for you.*

Words, theories, or lessons learned by rote and re-peated in order to pass academic examinations, thus un-derstood with the intellect alone, are far from being "pearls of wisdom." They are more like mathematical formulas for solving problems. For example, we have learned and intel-lectually understood many lessons about love and com-passion, and we have countless books filled with formulas that will help us "be in touch with our feelings" or behave more lovingly. These may be in the form of prayers, the practice of positive thinking, or any of the how to's of the New Age movement. Most of them aim at resolving the problems caused by our anger, frustration, and violence. In general, we as humanity have been able to pass on lessons from generation to generation through religion, intellectual discourse, mores, etc.; still we are a planet in trouble.

> ✿ *Have you observed that* **in general**
> *people have been helped by lessons only*
> *temporarily? Has this happened to you?*

I am not going to present psychological explanations or attempt to solve one individual's problems or those of hu-manity. This book is a process in human consciousness, an inquiry into the content of our present awareness. The pro-cess of questioning, probing into every convolution of our conditioned brains, may bring about a different kind of ac-tion, not as a solution to our problems, but rather as a new way of functioning in human consciousness. This distinct approach is *not* an attempt to find solutions within the same patterns of thinking that brought about the problems in the first place.

Humanity is on a problem-solving treadmill. This problem-solving approach to the material world has become a mind-set. We seem to believe that peoples' abilities to solve problems reflects their great capacity for survival on the planet. Indeed, our technological genius bears this out unequivocally. Yet we are blind to the consequences of our "solutions."

Of course, not all solutions bring about discomfort or misery. Many scientists, inventors, philosophers and religious leaders have helped to alleviate afflictions in our existence. We are not belittling the work of all the beautiful, dedicated people of this world whose contributions have benefited humanity through the ages.

> ✿ *How have you been helped? Have you resolved your problems? Do you feel the changes in your life have been limited and temporary or radical and lasting? Be thorough in your investigation.*

Conditioning Equals Continuity

The content of our minds has tremendous influence on our life-style, health, and relationships. Furthermore, due to the "conditionability" of the human organism, each of us registers in our brain our cultural patterns, or engrams. This is the basic content of the mind of our ancestors and of our contemporaries.

"Conditionability" (my neologism) here means the ability of the body to be conditioned, as a result of endogenous functioning. We see this propensity within the structure and functions of all the organs of the body.

In order to be conditioned from childhood we must be inherently predisposed to conditioning. Indeed, the human organism has the capability to habituate both mentally and physically.

Physically we can readily become habituated to substances such as alcohol, tobacco, and cocaine. Our bodies have natural responses to certain chemicals; for many people the response takes the form of craving for more of the same. Research with rhesus monkeys shows the same conditionability in these animals.

Mentally, we are conditioned through social attitudes. We learn and repeat behavior. Our brains are excellent computer like organs. We are conditioned through phrases such as "Knowledge is power" or "You must get an education to succeed in the world" or "You must honor and defend your country." We follow through by attending college, fighting for our rights, and going to war.

> ❦ *Can you look, gently, at humanity at large to see this predicament? Do you experience your own conditionability? For the time being, look in generalities. We will deepen our inquiry later.*

Our usual way of behaving, then, is predicated on our cultural conditioning, personal past experiences, and accumulated knowledge. Conditioning, the ever-needed process of acculturation, has remained an *unexamined* force in the development of all societies. Social scientists have not adequately factored conditionability into the development of civilizations. So humanity remains trapped in circles of conditioning, repeating and repeating patterns of behavior such as territoriality, aggression, and war.

The content of the collective mind of humanity remains the frame of reference for action, and ultimately it is a blueprint for our civilization.

Seeing Past Our Conditioning

Due to the conditioned state of the mind, reading this book objectively may be rather difficult. Yet this is exactly what is recommended. Each person must perceive the symbols appearing on these pages as an *active living experience*. It also means that intellectual or emotional understanding is not necessary, nor is it necessary to remember what is read.

> ✿ *The benefit of this approach is in the awareness of your experience at the moment of inquiry. You are experiencing not just for yourself, but for humanity as a whole!*

Holistic inquiry is very different from individual questioning. These two views actually arise from two dissimilar dimensions of consciousness. The personal view is limited while the holistic is all-encompassing. The personal is analogous to looking at a single planet or star, ignoring its relationship and similarity to the rest of the celestial bodies. The holistic view is akin to looking at the universe in its totality, as we can perceive it—the galaxies, suns, planets, black holes, all moving in relationship simultaneously, all influencing one another.

This general or holistic view is very confrontational for some of us. It demands that we see thoroughly and equally within ourselves all that we consider ugly and negative, as well as that which is brilliant and beautiful. This does not mean that everyone in the world is behaving or feeling all the negativity being exposed in this book. It simply means that we are, all of us, involved in the general movement of this human energy, without total awareness. It is our job to bring the negativity gently into consciousness without resistance. To deny our participation in that which we consider negative is to separate ourselves from the rest of our species. And once we do that, my friend, there goes our oneness!

> ✿ *Can you confront yourself as humanity?*
> *Since you and I cannot communicate*
> *verbally with all other human beings on*
> *the planet, we have to confront our own*
> *totality as "being everyone else."*
> *Compassionately, please!*

We experience ourselves mostly as separate entities. The concept of oneness remains in the realm of belief in religion and in the New Age movement. This concept of the interrelationship of everything in nature has been confirmed by quantum physics. We know, intellectually, that we are one.

If we were truly living an experience of oneness, we would see ourselves as humanity rather than as an individual "me." We may have an emotional or intellectual knowledge of oneness, but behave as separate "me's."

In our society, the urge to preserve this "me" supersedes the impulse to preserve the species. Living oneness would bring about a much needed sense of well-being in all of us. We would live cooperatively rather than competitively; we would not have rivalries or wars. Living oneness would be a transformation in itself.

In working with hundreds of people throughout the years, I have come to understand clearly the benefits of *seeing* oneself as humanity in daily living. Dr. James, a physician, comes to mind. She complained, "After forty years of acquiring knowledge and twenty years of workshops and lectures about self-improvement, I am still looking for the experience of unconditional love. It is very discouraging!" She was determined to live a life of love and oneness; she had retired from her profession and felt free to dedicate all her energies to the exploration of consciousness. After several months of talking about the human predicament and probing into her own conditioning, she realized how she had separated herself from others through her self-improvement training. She said, "I believed I was in Christ-consciousness, in oneness, but at the same time I felt at a higher plane than others. How could I have been so blind? No wonder I couldn't experience unconditional love; I thought I was better than others. I expected so much." There is no true love in separateness.

After experiencing herself *whole*—undivided and feeling her *humanness* at the core of her being—she said, "I cannot believe the way my life has turned around." Today she lives a joyful, giving life, serving others lovingly and without expectation.

Is Self-Improvement an Improvement?

Most people want to obtain something, be it peace of mind, salvation, happiness, riches, or the ability to get along with their families and co-workers. In order to satisfy these wants, a good number go endlessly to workshops, lectures, and "intensives." Many seek entertainment through attending seminars on the incredibly wide range of subjects available today—sex, abundance, prosperity, cleansing and healing—you name it.

Paying large sums of money for these different awareness techniques, they hope to hit upon one that will do the trick and make them confident, rich, enlightened, or whatever they may crave. In pursuit of these goals, they go to psychologists, teachers, gurus, and preachers; they read hundreds of books and follow the advice of experts.

People get involved so easily with these many new movements and fads—all offering so-called improvement and salvation—because of the enticements and promises to fulfill their needs. There is a wide assortment of opportunists, many of whom wish only to capitalize on human gullibility and frailty. Of course, some of these purveyors really believe in their own methods and products and think they are the only ones who have all the answers. This has been evident from the days of the patent medicine charlatans to some contemporary television preachers who are in trouble with the law, as well as the channelers who advise people where to live and what to buy.

I do not want to belittle the numerous courses, workshops, and conferences that may have a valuable impact on the lives of some people. Also, many individuals can be deeply touched by a book, person, or religious belief—but they are a minority. The prevailing majority of humanity does not enjoy these beautiful experiences or adopt a peaceful, healthy way of living. I have met many individuals who, after a decade of self-improvement, have realized that there is something beyond the self-enhancement techniques. They are often frustrated and wish to come to a daily way of living that is peaceful and loving. The following letter from Jean exemplifies this:

> While working in the peace movement, I found myself one day in the office of my representative to Congress, literally screaming in his face as he calmly stated, "The Russians are different than we are. They don't want peace, so we cannot trust them. " How could he believe that? As I left his office, I saw that I was neither peaceful nor loving. I realized that, just as my congressman felt different and separate from the Russians, so I felt different and separate from him. I thought about my behavior and said to myself, "This is where war begins. " All the self-improving, all the work I had done on myself for so many years, had not prepared me for the experience of myself as the other, as humanity itself. It had not dealt with my own divisions. The vio-

lence of humanity had been denied, avoided, buried in my own breast. My efforts at self-improvement were, in the context of humanity, like an aspirin taken for a headache, an amelioration of little personal sufferings, which helped me to distance myself from the larger sufferings of humankind. Self-help, self-improvement, can be a dangerous drug we use to obliterate our awareness of what is really happening in humanity. Comfort, solace, is obtained at the price of blindness to the whole, and to that unwanted truth about ourselves. You, Ligia, have continuously pointed to the truth, and I realize that it's up to me to look or not.

✿ *Please inquire into self-improvement technology and courses. Are the teachers living their teachings?*

Recently a young man came to dialogue about his future. He had stopped selling real estate because he felt he was not serving people in a totally honest way. Furthermore, he had quit his last job, in which he had taught "management improvement" to other companies. "I could not see teaching a course that we could not apply even in our own company; I could not stand what was going on among the employees. It was all so false," he bitterly complained. Even as he was coming to grips with his own integrity and honesty, he felt lost and uncertain about the future. When his ongoing process of discovery, which was already occurring, was reflected to him, his spirits lifted. He realized he had been teaching what he had *learned* while not being able to live it. All the improvement courses he had taken could not compare with his natural ability to discover, on his own, what was not working for him or his fellow humans. He recognized his inner conflict and at the same time his integrity, his truth—and now he was ready to honor this.

Civilization: An Improvement in Our Way of Living?

Our way of living seems essentially the result of a learning process, which consists of acquiring information and then retrieving and applying this knowledge whenever applicable. To enhance our security and comfort, we utilize the knowledge gained from our interaction with and manipulation of the physical world, and we are constantly refining that knowledge. The learning process is directed at living more affluently, with more pleasure and less pain; at possessing more things, more power, fame, or prestige. All these goals are common in our civilization, especially in the Western world, are they not?

> ✿ *Please look for yourself. This is your own investigation. Have you ever observed human behavior without considering what you may have learned about it previously? This is the kind of approach suggested here: to inquire within yourself anew.*

So now, after all the many years of striving for improvement, what kind of civilization have we developed? For example, we have made great technological strides in transportation, communications, and space research. We have been to the moon and back, probed other planets, and developed powerful weapons. Cars and computers are plentiful, making things easier for the scientist as well as for the laborer and the homemaker. Machines have reduced the need for manual labor. In medicine, we have conquered many diseases, including polio, diphtheria, and smallpox. We live longer and in more comfort, and we enjoy adult toys and varied entertainment. However, only a small minority enjoys the most luxurious and grand variety of technological wonders.

We cannot say that these are truly hard times for most of us. The Western world, in general, enjoys affluence. It is wonderful to be able to see the world while traveling in comfort, taking pleasure cruises or vacations by jet plane. There is so much beauty to appreciate! So many wonderful people all over the globe to meet!

We can be thankful for these wonderful experiences made possible by our own intelligent inventions. It is fascinating and most practical to use the different mechanical aids in our kitchens and workshops. Microbiologists have produced beautiful hybrid flowers and larger, different, and delicious fruits. In general we have an easier and better life. It seems as though we do not have much to complain about—or so we think!

> ❦ *Keeping fresh in your mind all the helpful and wonderful accomplishments, look carefully and without negativity at the* **consequences** *of some of these achievements.*

To begin with, on the global level, as a result of our knowledge of physics and chemistry, we now have pollution, atomic waste, and the possibility of this civilization coming to an end through the use of nuclear weapons. Other consequences of this progress are the emergence of new diseases as a result of the growing resistance of bacteria to drugs; pesticides often resolve one problem only to create another, larger one; large chemical and drug industries have thrived as a result of our "solutions" to problems. Furthermore, in the affluent nations there is considerable overeating. Businesses flourish on the sale of pills, herbs, exercise plans, and fad diets. Promoters of workshops and television programs are realizing big profits. According to some reports, alcoholism and drug abuse are common among adults and even among children eleven to thirteen years of age and younger. These problems are fostered and exploited by very profitable legal (tobacco and alcohol) and illegal (cocaine and designer drugs) businesses.

> ❦ *Please look meticulously at those state-ments. They are very strong and may appear accusatory. Do you see them as facts? I do not expect you to agree or disagree. Would you question the state-ments? How do they make you feel? Do you feel like accusing someone or de-fending yourself? It is my intention that you be aware of all your emotions, feel-ings and thoughts. A complete aware-ness of your experience brings you to the core of humanness. Let us continue.*

At this point you might be saying, "But not everybody has these problems," and you are right! Not everybody is engaged in escape through drugs, overeating, or exploiting others. Remember, we are looking at the very worst aspects of our civilization, and at our so-called progress and its effect on the quality of living in general.

It seems as though every time humanity resolves a problem, the solution then becomes another problem—a pattern that is repeated throughout time. A good example of this is the automobile. Undeniably it was a great im-provement over the horse and buggy. However, with this wonderful piece of machinery came the immense problems of the workers in the car industry. Then came pollution, a situation still inadequately controlled, plus the thousands killed and injured every year in automobile accidents. An

overall look at history clearly shows that, with its technological miracles, the great industrial revolution brought
conflict, violence, and misery for the masses.

> ✿ *Please look for yourself at the problem-*
> *solution situation, without agreeing or*
> *disagreeing, as if you had never heard of*
> *this before. This is a "now" that has*
> *never existed and will never again exist.*

Looking at these facts of our times, it is easy to fall into
a belief that we should go back to the horse and buggy
stage of development. This is not the proposal. On the
contrary! We need to come to realize that we must be more
aware of the consequences of our new technologies. We
are very intelligent beings playing with the fire of our own
genius! Many believe we are actually better off than we
were before in some ways. For example, we have abolished
slavery and child labor and our society is becoming
racially integrated. If we rest on our laurels, however, we
will fall asleep once again. This we cannot afford, my
friends. The greenhouse effect, due to pollution, and the
danger of nuclear holocaust are just two of the very real
threats that demonstrate the need for an awakening of
humanity.

> ✿ *If you're an optimist, let me challenge*
> *you. How are we better, overall? Think*
> *humanity—totally, please! I want to em-*
> *phasize the need for* **greater conscious-**
> **ness.**

Many thousands of individuals are enjoying the
achievements of civilization. Perhaps you and I are very
lucky and blessed by our positions or wealth, or simply by
having plenty to eat and a comfortable place to live. But
we can no longer ignore the millions who are hungry or

have no shelter, or those who live in violent environments.

> ✿ *Please gently acknowledge, without*
> *pride , blame or guilt, whether any of the*
> *above is true for you, This* **holistic** *in-*
> *quiry may bring perturbing feelings*
> *such as deep sadness or anger, my*
> *friends. This is an integral part of the*
> *process. Are you willing to experience*
> *this bleak outlook even though it may*
> *not apply to you personally? Look*
> *gently, compassionately.*

Our responsibility is to examine and experience, without condemnation, the facts about humanity as a whole. We are exploring the state of consciousness as it is on the planet in order to discover that which is beyond, that which is unmanifest to us.

CHAPTER THREE

Individuals:
Holograms of Humanity

If we could see an individual and all the peoples of the world simultaneously, the hologrammatic quality of humanity would be clearly apparent. A hologram is a three-dimensional photographic image obtained with laser beams; one small segment contains the whole picture. The most peculiar quality of a hologram is that when only a tiny part of it is broken off and projected, it shows an image of the entire object. Analogously, each person is the reflection of humanity and vice versa. All individuals are intricate parts of humankind. Each individual is a *whole* rather than a fragment of humanity.

If we look closely, we will be able to see this holo-grammatic quality of our personal life in our civilization. Observing objectively, we can see that each one of us *is* the world; each one of us *is* the whole of humanity. In other words, we—yes, you and I—are the source of our civilization, and we are therefore directly responsible for the quality of our way of living.

Humanity has survived through a process of learning and adaptation. We acquire information from the moment we are born, even from the way we are handled physically, and we retain it in our memory. Some people maintain this process starts prenatally. Information is passed on from generation to generation; thus, traditions, customs, and all types of repetitive behavior are developed and preserved by humankind in different cultures throughout the world.

Acculturation to Conflict

"Acculturation" is the ongoing process of conditioning a child to the patterns of society.

Our planet is divided into nations, each with its own particular program of conditioning. Although nations display many differences in their cultures, most of them have certain important elements in common—such as competitiveness and aggressiveness, witnessed in the worldwide competition in business and in the struggles for political and military power. Each country has its own general ideology—capitalism, socialism, communism, democracy, totalitarianism, or a combination of these—and some are striving for superiority, seeking to persuade other countries to change their own particular way of thinking and living. *Ideology, in some nations, has become more important than humanity.*

These divisive influences perpetuate the separation of people from one another and serve to maintain the different nationalities of the world. This territorial or tribal way of thinking has endured for thousands of years and persists to date in our civilization and in each one of us.

> ✿ *Please look at your own sense of territorial protectionism and how it affects others. Have you ever asked yourself how it is that most of us feel that we be-*

long to one country in particular rather
than to the world at large? Are we not
really citizens of this planet Earth?

Throughout the world human beings have evolved with competition, dividing themselves into races by skin color and other superficial physical features and into citizens of countries carrying their respective labels, such as British, Russian, and American.

These societies, in turn, are divided into classes—upper, lower, and middle; white-collar and blue-collar—or into castes, as in India. One might argue that some of these divisions are now disappearing; we have nondiscrimination laws in this country, and the strict caste system in some parts of India has relaxed. However, discrimination and bigotry persist only too often at the individual level as a result of traditional prejudices.

Due to people's striving for power and self-interest, most countries are divided politically between the right and left, Republican and Democrat, and so on. Religious divisions are manifold. People have separated into major religions such as Christianity, Judaism, Islam, Buddhism, and Hinduism, and these are further subdivided into numerous sects. Each group is bound to its particular beliefs, some claiming to have the only correct way toward salvation or enlightenment. These beliefs are sometimes given precedence over the action of true love.

Because of divisions we are always in conflict, fighting each other all over this planet. Forty wars are being fought at the present time. We are living in chaos and closing our eyes to it!

Essentially, human beings are the same everywhere, with the same emotions—fear, desire, greed, hope, hate, love. There is no difference in basic structure. We are all made of blood, flesh, and bone; we have the same organs; and we all think and feel, if not exactly alike, then along the same basic themes.

When working as a health professional and while traveling, I encountered people from all over the world. On an emotional level, women and men complain about one another, regardless of their country of origin, and with the same fervor they express their love and passions. Mothers and fathers everywhere fret about the future of their children and worry about the easy availability of alcohol and drugs to their young. Men and women alike compete in the marketplace for better-paid jobs. Furthermore, they compete and fight with equal intensity for territory or for power and economic status. They live with stress brought about by their life-style and by the pressures of modern business.

> ❦ *Are you different? Is there any competi-*
> *tiveness, aggressiveness, or tension in*
> *your daily living? Keep looking at your-*
> *self as humanity.*

We have been observing the divisions in the world at large; let us now look more closely at the smaller units which make up our society. In businesses, religions, schools, and government, the same problems arise. For example, management and labor, being in an inherently adversarial relationship, are hardly ever in agreement. And the situation is not much different between fellow worshippers, teachers and students, politicians and constituents. They also are at odds with one another, competing or fighting over the most trivial issues. Cooperation seems to be based mainly on self-interest— "I'll scratch your back if you'll scratch mine."

> ❦ *Where do you fit into the pattern of sep-*
> *aratism in humanity? Have you looked*
> *at these common occurrences as being*
> *consequences of our own divisions?*
> *Remember, this is your own investiga-*

*tion. These questions are simply a stim-
ulus pointing to the way it is, without
expectations of changing your way of
thinking.*

The still smaller units of society—for example, the family—frequently share the fate of the world at large, namely, a life of conflict!

Many psychotherapists and counselors deal with psychological problems; we have specialists in the field of family therapy attempting to resolve disputes, incompatibilities, sibling rivalry, and so on. Child abuse, wife beating, and crimes of passion are rife in the so-called civilized world. If you look at the divorce rate, you'll see that there has been very little improvement in family relationships over the years. Men and women, regardless of their education or religious upbringing, have not yet learned to get along with each other.

> ✤ *This kind of family turmoil may or may
> not apply to you personally. Please look
> at the larger picture. You are looking for
> those who are unwilling to look for
> themselves, as well as for yourself.*

Finally, let us talk about the very smallest unit of society, the individual human being. We are going to observe ourselves directly and see if there are divisions within ourselves.

Conflict Within Ourselves

Regardless of how we actually are, we have, according to our upbringing, been given a distinct idea, or perhaps two or three, of how we "should be." We have all been acculturated. We have all been cast into a particular mold, to which we may have conformed in order to survive in society. This mold is determined by our societal mores and beliefs, and by the ideals or particular religious beliefs of our own family.

So there is the *way we are*, and then there is the *way we should be*; thus we are set up for division. If this were not so, would we feel a desire to improve ourselves? Would we need organizations to tell us how to be? This internal, individual division creates conflict within each of us. We feel and behave in a certain way, yet worry all the time about the way we *should* feel and behave. Our notion of how we should be is often dictated by those we admire, emulate, compare ourselves to, or imitate. Sometimes the conflict arises when we compare yesterday's activities or their results with today's—and we end up competing with ourselves for a better performance day after day. If the should-be's are not realized, we feel frustrated and unhappy.

> ✾ *What are the should-be's in your life? Are you trying to improve yourself according to some standard, belief, or authority? Or perhaps you have revolted and feel you are now your own person, different from others in your milieu. Look at your facts. There is no intention of judgment in our observation.*

We seek out teachers and gurus to help us put ourselves together. We are so thoroughly conditioned that we assume we ought to live in a certain way—without ever questioning our basic assumptions. The following case exemplifies this human predicament.

John Lee had worked on a military base for years. He enjoyed living in a small town with his wife, their three children, and two grandparents. But all through the years John had a vague feeling that something was wrong inside him. He did not know exactly what it was, since everything was going smoothly in his life. He went through periods of sadness and preoccupation about the weapons being used at the base. But John was "doing his duty," and he realized that the weapons were necessary for national defense. He had position, prestige, a great family, and money.

When he was in the garden of his beautiful house, he felt great joy working with the flowers and experiencing the beauty of nature. His joy would frequently turn to a sadness, however, when he thought of his profession. He wished he could quit! But he would have had to forgo too much seniority, too many benefits for himself and his family. He was now forty years old and, despite Christian religious training, diligent efforts at self-improvement, and much knowledge about meditation and unconditional love, he realized he had "gotten nowhere." He began a deep exploration into his own conditioning.

He was in conflict. There was, in his words, "a battle between his heart and his mind." He had done all he should do, according to his upbringing, but he had never followed his true inner nature and wishes. After he realized just how close he had come to being a total automaton of social mandates, he began to experience his own caring and love for others. He eventually quit his job and began a garden service business. Today he is successful and free of conflict from old "should's," following his heart and serving people by doing work that he really enjoys. His experience of universal love, he says, has truly deepened.

Like John Lee, many of us live our lives without ever really questioning our training or our background, and without seeing the power of acculturation. We are unaware of the wonderful peace of mind and joy we are missing.

Perhaps we have been too blind or too afraid to go through this process of investigating and giving up old patterns. Being afraid to suffer more, we remain stuck in our old *familiar* suffering. We are robbing ourselves of great joy because of *fear*.

> ✿ *Can you look at your own life and see if you are following your heart? Are you dissatisfied with your way of living? Are you afraid to change? Look gently, without reprimanding yourself or feeling pride! Just look!*

Persistent Competitiveness

We have talked about competition in the world at large and at the national level. The same drive, or feeling, or whatever motivational label you use, predominates also at the individual level—human beings are holograms of humanity. Further separating from one another, we strive for better jobs or a better position in society, trying to acquire more of anything—money, property—or even greater spiritual achievement, perhaps trying to levitate or to be enlightened. Competition in spiritual concerns is apparent when one hears practitioners of certain forms of meditation say, "My mantra is really more powerful," "My guru or my religion is the only way to salvation," and so on.

> ✿ *We are not criticizing religious leaders, or their followers. We are simply looking at what is. Do you feel your point of view to be the only valid one, or do you think it is only one of many correct ones? Are you an atheist or a believer? Do you feel this is the best way to be, or is it simply the only way you know? Are you repeating what you have learned? Keep investigating.*

What I am suggesting here is that you see holistically. As we are observing, individual behavior essentially repeats itself on the national and international levels.

> Individual Conflict
> National Conflict
> World Conflict

All of this expresses chaos. How can we pretend to bring order at the world and national levels when our own house is in disorder?

> ✿ *One needs to be extremely careful not to judge or evaluate! Remember, this is merely a way of **looking** and therefore strictly neutral. Likewise, any comments your mind may have on these writings are to be observed. Is this a part of your experience? Find out!*

Looking at our collective global problems is discouraging, even depressing. We have to be careful *not* to be negative in our emphasis on the disorder. We need to explore, realizing that our willingness to confront things *as they are* indicates that a shift is already occurring in our consciousness.

> ✿ *Have you noticed that you are concerned sufficiently about humanity to read a book supporting this process of direct, deep inquiry?*

Indeed, many people in the world are intensely concerned with the lack of awareness in humanity. We are occasionally awake enough to see that our predicament is a matter of quality of consciousness. This was apparent in the 1989 conference of a group of psychologists and health professionals and the Dalai Lama of Tibet. The participants' overriding concern was harmony in the world. They were very candid in their exploration of subjects such as compassion, anger, and violence. All of those on the panel were honest about personal experiences of discontent, perplexity, sadness, and the apparent hopelessness of the human predicament. At the same time, there was an awareness of the need to confront these issues compassionately. All participants recognized the need for a deep look at themselves and humanity without judgment or evaluation.

Yet even in this gathering the insidious problem-solving approach, based on our traditional ways of thinking, was present. In this wonderful atmosphere of sincerity and compassion, the traditional suggestions of what to do retained their invisible force. Our conditioning is so tenacious that it takes great energy to confront the truth of it. The mind "gets around itself." For example, while speaking about conditioning, we miss the fact that it is through this same conditioning to a language that we are able to speak. This was so at the conference as it is in our daily living.

It is very important to remain aware of one's own limitations. It is just as imperative that we do not become overly concerned or worried about being conditioned.

> ✿ *The process of this book, my friend, is demanding. Take your time! It is your process of inquiry. You are the one who can see yourself in the context of humanity as humanity itself. Letting your mind be confused or perturbed by anything in this book is part of the process. Out of respect for your own wisdom, I am not giving many explanations or offering solutions.*

Summary

These early chapters have been an exploration and exposition of the extreme afflictions of the world at large. We have seen the following:

1. A hologrammatic quality is inherent in human beings.
2. While we are not personally to blame for creating great problems in the world, we remain responsible as part of the hologram of humanity.
3. Each person's experience in the consciousness of the world is important.
4. The exploration into the unfavorable side of human beings, while perturbing, is imperative in order to raise our general consciousness; our survival depends on it.
5. Our own functioning, abilities, and intelligence have produced adverse consequences.
6. Without total awareness, intelligence is dangerous.
7. We need a different consciousness to continue to progress technologically without creating larger problems.
8. The adverse forces of conditioning are strong, but that conditioning is a necessity for survival in society.
9. There are divisions and incongruity in our own makeup.
10. Finally, conflict is repetitive within the individual and in the world.

We have emphasized the most unpleasant consequences of our civilization throughout these writings because they graphically illustrate the great need for a *radical* change in consciousness. We explored facts we often try to ignore in order to avoid pain. Indeed, the truth of our predicament is most disturbing to us. Too many people are unable to experience love, joy, and harmony in relationships. We need to transcend our predicament.

Through these chapters we have brought into our particular awareness the general consciousness, or rather *unconsciousness*, of the majority of people on the planet. Human beings must discover their process of transformation and honor their cocoon-like stage.

Collectives:
The Structure of Consciousness

Thought-Memory

According to what we have examined, to see the individual is to view humanity as a whole. This allows us to see the hologrammatic quality of human beings: a single individual, organization, or society, although forming only a part of the picture, contains the whole of humankind.

"Each one is the world!" If you have heard this before, please do not just agree or disagree. Wait! Let us ask, "Has this civilization resulted from the interaction of very different individuals, or has it evolved from a commonality in all individuals?" Let us examine this issue carefully.

The human body, anatomically and physiologically, is exactly the same, within the sexes, regardless of skin color or racial features. We are, essentially, *a specific arrangement of molecules*, which forms the physical basis of an emotional and mental process.

We receive information, which is retained in memory. This is the basis of the thought-memory process—the accumulative learning process. Through generations, we amass knowledge, upon which we build and elaborate, developing traditions and customs. But this accumulation means that we repeat and repeat *and repeat*, conditioned by the past.

We need to question if this thought-memory function lies at the root of the evolution of civilization; and we need to see if it is the basis for the similarity in the way human beings behave all over the world. We have ourselves been educated by means of repetitive behavior, and we continue to educate our children this way. For example, if we are nationalistic, we train our young people to kill for our country or our territory. This behavior persists in humanity and today it is no different than it was in primitive times. It is not basically different from animals fighting over territory!

> ✾ *Please see the facts! We are not criticizing nationalism; we are looking at ways of thinking and the consequences that have persisted through generations. Each one of us is looking at our behavior and beliefs, and doing so objectively.*

People learn many do's and don't's from their elders or from experts, and believing these authorities, they follow blindly—repeating behavior even when it is not fundamentally in their own best interests.

> ✾ *Do you believe human beings have progressed in consciousness, as they think they have? How do you see it?*

Our consciousness consists of that which we have learned from our ancestors and contemporaries; this is so for all humans in the world. Is the thought-memory process the basis for human beings' state of consciousness? Or is it the basis for the content of consciousness?

🌹 *Have you ever investigated this? What is the content of your consciousness?*

The content of our consciousness differs from person to person and from culture to culture. The state of consciousness refers to the mental condition of being aware.

Thought-memory is at the basis of the content of consciousness. It is what facilitates the ongoing process of acculturation. In order to pass on information, customs, beliefs, and traditions, we need memory as well as the ability to abstract.

🌹 *How do you experience memory? What is it? When you recall something, are you thinking? Please look.*

The question of thought or thinking seems logically to follow in our inquiry. What is the nature of thought? The obviously physical aspect of thought is that of electrical impulses traveling through the nervous system. (This is an extreme simplification of the scientific findings.) The psychological (subtle) aspect is the content of thought. It is this subtle aspect that is of interest to us here.

Awareness of Thought

What is the content of thought? What does thought refer to in general (not the particular subject)? Does thought concern the past? the present? the future?

🌹 *Have you noticed your own thoughts? Are they about the past or future? Stop and look! Right now, what is your thought?*

It may be obvious that the content of thought can *only be past or future*, even if that past or future is just an instant before or after the fact. Take notice that by the time we think of anything (evaluate, compare, etc.), we are already in the past. If we are *thinking* of changing something, we are into the future as well as the past.

> ✿ *Can you be at observation right now, without saying yes or no to the statement?*

Is thought only past or future? Is thought possible because we retain all we perceive?

> ✿ *Have you ever asked yourself what causes thought? How it arises? What stimulates it? Are you not thinking right now? You can leave this book at any moment and simply ponder the matter without answering the questions. Have you done this with other books? Perhaps you are tired of this questioning, but we entered into an inquiring relationship, did we not?*

Scientists cannot prove how, or that, babies think. However, they are able to detect traces of brain activity involved in thought. An electroencephalogram attests to this activity. Despite all the research, however, we are still unaware of the true origin of the thinking function. Yes, there are many theories, just as there are many hypotheses of the origin of man and of the universe. Nevertheless, the more discoveries we make, the more we see our ignorance.

We may say with certainty that we are cognizant of our thinking process. But are we truly aware of thinking at the very moment it occurs, an awareness that is not another thought?

🌹 *Perhaps you can look directly into this
quandary: "Awareness of thinking is
not another thought."*

If answers are coming, but not from what we have
learned, we may simply be insightful! Insight differs from
thought arising from memory. It is a spontaneous awareness, and its origin is usually inexplicable.

The Inherent Divisiveness of Thought

Observing thought very carefully, we can see that it is,
by its own nature, divisive. It divides everything into opposites—good-bad, love-hate, and so forth. It measures
psychologically in the same way that it measures physically—tall-short, up-down, comparing and evaluating.
Therefore, it separates the "you" from the "me," comparing and measuring one human against another. It also divides the individual within him or herself. We are all ac-
quainted with statements like these: "A part of me wants
to have it, and the other part says no," and "I am good
sometimes, but at other times something gets hold of me."

🌹 *Can you see the divisive nature of
thought? Is there a division of different
"me's" in your own experience?*

As long as we separate ourselves within, we will produce a fragmented society; consequently we will continue
to divide humankind into religions, nationalities, and races.
The *me* will continue to be important, as will the entire
ideology of "my home, my country," and so on. In this
manner, poverty and brutal wars will inevitably persist,
since division ever breeds conflict. On the other hand, in
"oneness"—not as a concept, but as an actuality—who is

there to compete with or to fight?

Our thought-memory process is divisive, and it is responsible for the content of our consciousness. It is about the past or the future. It is a function that facilitates acculturation and the continuity of traditions, conflict, pleasures, addictions, and so on. It is also the greatest tool of our intelligence.

Transformation Beyond Thought

Our memory-thought process facilitates learning from experts such things as mathematics, physics, and religion. It even helps us learn about ourselves. We explain our actions through knowledge of psychology and the social sciences.

We seem to have learned very little about our essential nature and the purpose of human existence, except through religious and philosophical studies or beliefs. There has been much talk and thousands of books have been written about this, as well as about the "transformation of humans." Followers of gurus who discourse on this subject are continuously trying to achieve this "shift" or "change" in their own consciousness.

In recent decades we have had a deluge of gurus from India, and many more of them are aspiring to come to rich America. On one of my journeys, I encountered a teacher in India who was very persistent in trying to persuade my tour group to take him to the United States. He insisted that he had a cure for cancer, and to please the crowd he even sang some popular American songs. It seemed rather inappropriate for this "saint," as he was called, to be singing "You Are My Sunshine." He promised transformation and Buddhahood; he vowed to cure diseases and change people's lives. He had all the trappings of a holy man, including an altar with the image of a goddess.

We could not have so many aspirants to the role of

teacher if we ourselves did not really crave authority, someone to tell us how to transform ourselves.

A transformational state, then, has become desirable, something that the brain has registered as a goal to be achieved. This necessarily has to be in the realm of thought-memory, which we know only too well. We practice and practice in order to achieve transformation. This proves a futile endeavor, a waste of energy, and ultimately a frustrating experience when the goals are not reached. Often the mind will then invent an experience that simulates the one described by the guru, giving us a false sense of having reached a state of higher consciousness. Yet the problems in our lives and our relationships continue, much to our chagrin!

The following conversation with someone who visited the Self-Studies Foundation depicts this predicament:

> **Questioner:** I have been practicing meditation and guided imagery for a long time. I have taught the techniques to my little daughter, and for a while it worked. Why is it that the magic seems to have stopped? How can she regain it?
> **Ligia:** Is the magic still with you but not still with your daughter?
> **Questioner:** Yes, it's pretty much with me.
> **Ligia:** Pretty much, meaning not all the time?
> **Questioner:** Yes, not all the time.
> **Ligia:** Is it not that way with your daughter also? It works, but not all the time?
> **Questioner:** Yes, it's the same.
> **Ligia:** So if it is not always with you, it is not always with your daughter. Were you not the one teaching the techniques?
> **Questioner:** Yes, I guess so. But my teacher said that as long as I used the techniques correctly, I would be always in a higher consciousness. I think my daughter and I are at a higher level

than we were, but we are still falling back and getting sick, and we don't always get better with visualizations.

Ligia: So this level of higher consciousness is like the old level—sometimes things work, other times they do not. I would question this higher consciousness.

Questioner: Hmmm.

Yet another case is that of Larry, who took a workshop with a well-known physician now doing spiritual work. At the workshop Larry related an experience he called *transcendental*. He was in the *void*. He felt he had left his body and was in this great void where white light permeated everything. There he experienced the unconditional love the doctor had spoken of earlier in the workshop. He said he felt transformed. Yet the next day Larry was observed in a hallway arguing with his wife and storming away, leaving a perplexed lady behind. There are countless cases of believers being frustrated because they confuse natural peak experiences of consciousness with a total change in consciousness.

Transformation, which implies a total and radical shift, can never occur through projecting goals and mechanically practicing these self-projected ideals. In other words, it does not happen through thinking.

Transformation needs to occur in the process of thought itself—that is, not *through* what we think but at the root of the thinking function. For this, a radical change is needed at the cellular level of the organism.

> ❦ *Please notice your own thought process. Observe the content of your thoughts: your goals, desires, and beliefs. This needs to be done neutrally, without judging your thoughts.*

The transformation process that gurus and teachers describe today may be only superficial changes within the same consciousness that we have always experienced and in which we remain. This consciousness is one of conflict and suffering, dedicated to the "me"—that is, the satisfaction of *my* personal desires, needs, and pleasures.

For human beings to be transformed, consciousness at large must be transformed. If we are explaining or understanding ourselves through knowledge from books or experts, we will continue to move within a conditioned consciousness. For transformation to occur, this movement has to stop!

The ending of this movement is what Eastern philosophers often refer to as the *silencing of the mind*—a task that has puzzled and frustrated many people. Quieting the mind is like trying to solidify quicksand with mud! For to *think* that we can stop thought is simply more thinking! Therefore, the present quality of thinking would have to end of its own accord, yet not through any *action* by thought itself.

Indirect Knowledge

The overall demeanor of humanity leaves us skeptical about the state of our consciousness and especially our awareness. We have observed the considerable technological achievements in communication, medicine, horticulture, and space travel. We have also observed the perennial problems of poverty, starvation, war, crime, child abuse, drug abuse—the list is long! And we think we are aware, awakening! Aware of what, my friends?

> ❦ *Please ask yourself this: looking anew, do you believe humanity is truly becoming more aware? Is it awakening? Find out for yourself, gently.*

Awareness is being on one's guard, vigilant, knowing or realizing, conscious, informed. Aside from the formal dictionary definition, the word "awareness" connotes expanded consciousness or expanded reality. It is often associated with awakening, a state that encompasses dimensions believed by some Eastern philosophers to be "beyond thought." It is this connotation that we need to examine carefully.

Perhaps by "aware " we mean that we are cognizant, that we have knowledge of things and situations—having been told about them or having perceived them. For example, I may have heard on the radio or in church about starving people, or I may have observed such people in person while traveling in India and Bangladesh. So I am cognizant of the problem. Now I have a remembrance of the situation and of the feelings it evoked in me. We retain, in our brains, the memory of emotions as well as thought. We *feel* bad about starving children when we *think* about them.

So we have some kind of awareness that is both intellectual and emotional. But do we realize that *knowing about* the world situation, *feeling bad about it*, or *being aware* of it has not changed human suffering? Do we see that the conditions ever remain the same? Starvation and wars continue, regardless of all the organized activity and the many, many altruistic people dedicated to combating hunger and poverty and working toward ending war.

> ❀ *Once more, please look deep within yourself as you read, see, or hear these things. Self-observation is unceasing. What are your inner reactions, thoughts, feelings, sensations? Just observe.*

The awareness we presently have is an indirect knowing acquired through information from others. What we call awareness seems actually to be cognizance, which Webster's dictionary defines as perception, or knowledge.

The majority of us listen to authorities or read books by experts to find out more about ourselves. We know ourselves only through the explanations of a Freud, a Piaget, or a Timothy Leary. We experiment on rats to theorize about the nature of human beings.

This is not a criticism of the experts or their research. They are there to teach us from their particular expertise. We can benefit from their knowledge of the physical world and they can help us live a more comfortable life. But reliance on experts pulls us ever further from knowing ourselves directly.

For years there has been research on human behavior and the mind; still, human beings know more about the moon! One wonders if the way we go about understanding ourselves is at all appropriate. Research into the mind and behavior is conducted in the same manner that the physical world is investigated—using thought, memory, and repetition in a cumulative fashion. This type of inquiry is inadequate, because it does not result in peace of mind or harmony for the majority of human beings.

> �֍ *Are you a researcher into yourself or merely in search of scientific explanations? What is your background? What knowledge have you acquired? Has it helped you to live harmoniously on a daily basis?*

Direct Knowledge

A question now arises: Is there a different way of knowing? We are not seeking information already documented and locked inside the computer brain. We are looking for a knowing that comes in a flash, that is so vital and complete that you know it to be firsthand and not just regurgitated from hearsay. You might call this spontaneous activity *insight* or *intuition*. We are referring to a way of knowing *outside of the system that registers and accumulates information.* In this instance, there is no judgment or evaluation, nor is there an evaluative comparison; it is just a very clear knowing.

Is it possible that there is direct self-observation, an immediate, total understanding of human nature—an observation that does not require the mediation of an authority or an expert?

Let us keep asking ourselves this: Is there such a way of seeing "what is" without choice, without resistance, without repetition, without judgment or evaluation, and without emotionality? (I use the word "emotionality " to mean an emotional state based on memory.) All of these are very important to consider, because such a perception would represent *objective seeing.*

Before proceeding, we need to understand what we accept as awareness—lest we fall victim to the same mechanical thought process in disguise.

We actually believe that we learn from our past experiences, history, or mistakes. Do we not commonly teach this to our children? But do we really learn from our past? And if so, when, and to what avail? There is a realm of knowledge in which this is absolutely true. In mathematics, science, and technology we learn from our mistakes, and we build and rebuild constantly upon the lessons we have learned. For this we need thought-memory.

But outside these areas, have we learned from human history? We certainly are aware of the misery brought about by territorial conflict. Still, this knowledge has not taught us to eliminate war.

> ❦ *Please observe this fact compassionately.*
> *Do not take these words as true or false.*
> *Take time to see for yourself.*

In spite of all our knowledge of the brutalities and devastation of warfare, world conflicts continue. Yet some authors suggest that today appears to be a time of awakening in the history of humanity. And indeed there is great interest in world peace, love, and service to others. However, the world has never been devoid of people dedicated to compassionate living and serving humanity. Still, what predominates is a dedication to the acquisition of material things and knowledge, the pursuit of pleasure, and the alleviation of pain.

Regardless of our much revered knowledge, our way of living continues to be based on separateness and territorial defense. In the 1960s, our youth were fed up with separatism and warfare. Their slogan, "Make love, not war," seemed to make an impact on many people's way of thinking—but not enough! Not enough!

Although we keep teaching and preaching love, it is still not abundant in humanity in proportion to the extent of activities by the religions, their doctrines, and their years of existence. Love has been preached from time immemorial, yet we continue to have religious wars to this day.

We need a totally new awareness, not based on traditional knowledge. We need a direct knowing based on wisdom, the wisdom of our hearts.

Self-Exploration:
The Moment of Insight

We must further ask: Is awareness—as in "New Age awareness"—repetitive thinking? Many people feel strongly that we are going through a transformation. But is this just a new belief? If so, it is only a change within the same consciousness that humankind has known for millennia.

Books and songs have been written about the Age of Aquarius, the Age of Enlightenment, and the new "conspiracy in awareness." Some authors truly believe that things in the world are improving as we enter a new age.

It is important to inquire for ourselves if this is not becoming another belief. If it is, we will simply be exchanging one kind of authority for another. Do we want to continue to learn about love, awareness, and peace of mind in the same manner that we learn about mathematics?

> ❦ *We are forever reading books on how to know ourselves. Please look at this slowly, carefully! Your life is your own*

book, the same as has been written many
times over! Would you read that book?

When someone points out something about human nature, we can listen and then investigate for ourselves. But if we automatically accept and repeat this observation, all we do is record and play back information. This is only a superficial understanding of ourselves.

From the viewpoint of a transformation, the conventional study of the intellectual and emotional makeup of human beings is insufficient, and the resulting knowledge is irrelevant. Regardless of all our psychological books and experiments, all our religious and philosophical doctrine, humanity still suffers.

What we have been discussing thus far is knowledge that is acquired and therefore secondhand; it comes from others and we merely repeat it. However, there is a way of knowing that is spontaneous, direct, and therefore firsthand—a self-knowing that does not originate in systems that hear, read, retain, and repeat. It is what we referred to earlier as *insight*, or *wisdom*; it is a *way of knowing* that is experienced as coming from other than the brain function of thinking. It is sometimes referred to as "the lighting of a light bulb," "clarity," or "sudden realization." It definitely has a different quality from analytical thought.

> ✿ *What does insight mean to you? Have*
> *you experienced sudden realization?*
> *What books have you read on the subject?*

Traditionally, through our way of thinking, we learn about ourselves via the experts, and acting from this we raise our children according to this book or that one. In the absence of books, we follow the way of our parents (our authorities), and thus we perpetuate certain patterns of behavior. Occasionally we rebel against tradition and develop a new trend which, being merely a reaction against the old pattern, is still bound by the past. Most of us can still remember our youth, our rebelliousness against or submission to the rules of our parents and teachers and the mandates of society.

The youth of today are rebelling by changing their dress code, as did previous generations. *It is the same psychological movement in different attire.* Slowly the new trend infiltrates the older generation, finally being absorbed and becoming the fashion of the day. An ever-changing outer look still masks the same repetitive pattern in the thinking process. The so-called new trend sometimes becomes traditional, and the same process repeats itself endlessly.

> ❦ *Have you looked at your conditioning? Have you noticed your way of thinking? The words spoken or printed are not important. Only your self-inquiry is of value.*

It is difficult for a mind to go beyond its limitations. "We cannot see the forest for the trees" is the perfect analogy for our state of consciousness. However, we must also remember that we are creatures of the universe, with potential to be the trees *and* see the forest. The process described in this book can be as powerful as an earthquake in the mind, breaking through the solid structures of conditioning.

> ❦ *This book is your process of inquiry. It is up to you to utilize this power that lies within you.*

Thus the appropriate question right now is: When are we going to let go of this secondhand manner of knowing and know ourselves directly? When?

❦ *When is humanity going to be free of this bondage? Will you question yourself right now? Without forcing, please!*

Objective Self-Observation

Knowing ourselves directly means we need to watch, look, or observe objectively our action in the moment. I am referring here to observation as an occurrence, a natural happening that does not originate in the thinking function. The term "objective observation" does not refer to a method or technique; it is a spontaneous process. The dictionary definition of the word "objective" applicable here is "without bias or prejudice; detached; impersonal."

Objective self-observation, then, is an observation that is neutral, unbiased, free of judgment and evaluation, detached from emotionality, and *independent of the mind's content*. In other words, it is independent of the already-known, the many acquired prejudices, evaluations of good and bad; and it is free of all "should be's." Objective self-observation is a way of looking at ourselves afresh, with nothing except *what is at the moment*. Notice that this is not analysis or comparison; it is not constructive criticism or evaluation based on a standard or norm.

Now the question is: Who or what does the observing? The mind? The brain, which has acquired so much know-how already? The system of thought that has invented all the technical things but has also caused havoc in the world? The system that learns and repeats?

❦ *Please see what is meant here. We are now observing "observation." We are looking deeply without our memories of what someone else may have said about any of this. Just watch and tell the truth about yourself now.*

So far we have observed that the brain has the ability to accumulate images and repeat behavior from memory. In a computer like fashion, the brain retains the remembrance of events, emotions, and thoughts for later output. Given this computerizing quality, objectivity (as this word is used here) cannot belong to the brain's functions of analysis and comparison. "Objective" here means "outside the mind's content." Therefore this objectivity cannot belong to the realm of thought; it belongs to the realm of *insight* or *wisdom*. Such a clear insight is a *spontaneous, unrepeatable event* that is not within the nature of thinking per se, since it is not based on past experience.

It is important to note that when we share this kind of realization, we are talking about the *verbalized memory of the experience of insight*; we cannot share insight itself. Objective self-observation is a uniquely clear and spontaneous knowing; we cannot teach it, acquire it, or practice it, for all of that belongs to the thinking process.

By now you might be saying, "Well, what is the use of even discussing it if we can *do nothing* toward experiencing insight or clarity within ourselves?" Well . . . .

> ✿ *What you are reading is meant simply to point out what is. Your own discovery is the real value of the experience. You may be insightful at any moment.*

Relationships in Humanity: Is There Objectivity?

The human race has divided this planet into countries, each with its own label—Japanese, American Russian. We relate to one another through these labels. The most important thing about them is that they are attached to learned emotions.

For example, during World War II many very young children heard their parents' emotional labels for the Japanese people. The word "Jap" became part of everyday language. Later, these children repeated phrases, such as "Japs are no good," voicing contempt for human beings they did not even know. They had retained *not only the label* but also the *feeling* attached to it—the latter being a learned response. This is what I have referred to as emotionality. In this way, we carry prejudices, opinions, and evaluations about one another. So when we meet and relate to others, how do we actually see them?

> ✿ *Each one of us is humanity. I keep repeating this statement over and over, not to bore you, but simply to remind you that our investigation is within the context of the whole.*

In listening to the news carefully, you may observe how thought functions through biases and labels. Newscasters, in reporting on politicians, lawbreakers, and other groups of people, often identify them by their skin color, nationality, or religion. For example, they report on the "black mayor of Chicago," the "Catholic senator," a "group of Chicanos," or a "mob of rioting blacks. " We do not hear about the "white mayor of Chicago" or a "mob of rioting whites." The news is supposed to be reported objectively, without emotion. However unemotional the voice of the person may be, the fact is that these labels carry associated unconscious memories of feelings, and these in turn evoke further emotions.

> ✿ *We are not criticizing newscasters. We are questioning the labels people use and the nature of thought-memory. This is your inquiry into conditioning.*

Thought is memory and it is reflected in our speech. So we have learned to label human beings and to separate them from one another. The moment we call ourselves Americans and point to others as blacks or Indians, we imply that they are not like us. It is the conscious or unconscious emotional associations that pass on prejudice from person to person and from generation to generation. Thus, the judgment and evaluation of human beings persists, overtly and covertly, in the world.

Words and emotions, then, are *retained in memory together,* for we remember the feelings as well as the labels attached. At times, each type of memory is stored separately; thus the remembrance of a word or a situation might be recorded in the brain separately from the emotion. Anna Freud lists many such examples in her book, *Mechanisms of Defense.*

We are conditioned according to our environment and nurturing, and from the very beginning of our lives we hold on to our learned experiences.

> ✿ *You can see this in yourself. Like everyone else, do you not feel, think, emote, memorize, and hold on to the past? Can you observe in yourself this conditioned process?*

The question now is this: Do we see each other through a network of thought, already established in the brain that has divided us into races, nationalities, the intellectuals, the privileged and the underprivileged, the authorities and the students, but never as just human beings?

> ✿ *We are referring not to the "other guy" but to ourselves. It is up to each one of us to answer this question. See yourself through your own eyes, unbiased, without any judgment or evaluation.*

It is the nature of the brain to function as a recorder. This is important in the survival of the human being. We need thought-memory to go from here to there, drive a car, learn language, and so forth. So we are not deprecating thought, nor are we belittling memory. We are simply examining our own modus operandi.

Self-Observation in Relationships

Let us now turn our attention to individual relationships. How do we relate to each other? Through remembrance of the past? Through the memory of what we did? We are looking at the thinking process carefully, observing the way we operate.

Let's use an example: For three years, my husband sent me flowers on our wedding anniversary. The fourth year, however, he forgot this date, which is so important to me that I remember vividly the wedding day, all the anniversaries, and all the flowers I have received. These memories are significant to me. When I receive flowers I am happy, and when I do not receive them I am hurt. My thinking drifts into doubts—"Does he still care for me?"—and of course I am upset!

Is the hurt just happening in my mind? We are not looking for psychological explanations or analyses, but just at the *fact* and the dynamics of my hurt.

Observing myself objectively, I see the following: for three consecutive years I received flowers on a certain date; the fourth year, on that date, the flowers did not arrive. That was all that happened, no more, no less. I can see that the presence or absence of flowers per se cannot inflict pain. What, then, is the cause of the psychological problem?

> ✿ Let us proceed slowly. If you have an
> answer in mind, please observe if it is an

answer from the known, the past. Then
you may want to let go of it and look
anew!

As I am interested in knowing myself, I will have this natural urge to be clear, to know, not from another—a priest, a psychologist, a counselor—but by myself, *now*, while I am hurting. This is my opportunity for objective self-observation. The situation (my husband's action) appears to be the cause of my discomfort. What makes this situation a real source of hurt for me?

I may have the following monologue: "How dare he forget, after all we have gone through together during these past four years? After all I have done for him, you would think he would be grateful that I married him. I thought he loved me." . . . And I note all of these thoughts going swiftly by, ever blaming, ever building, and forever registering themselves in my brain.

So I begin to inquire further: "My husband did not send flowers this year. How can this action directly hurt me? I am not being abused or insulted. He has not said anything to offend me. Why do I feel so upset just because he forgot our anniversary? He forgets many things. Am I angry at his lack of memory? What is truly going on? Did I expect him to remember in the same way I expect myself to remember things? Of course I am always disappointed when I do not live up to my expectations . . . . Oh! Wait a minute!" My mind says his action hurt me; however, I see clearly that my husband did not cause the pain. Still, I am disappointed and upset. So I ask myself if my expectations were the crucial factor.

If I realize that my feeling of being let down is the result of my expectations, then I will begin to see my thought-memory system at work. The flowers signified his love for me; and the yearly repetition of this was his assertion of caring. I hold on to the memory of the wedding and previous anniversary bouquets, and from them I develop my expectations. Also, I have compared my memories of the recent event with the images I hold of my husband— the way I *think* he should be.

Obviously, thoughts and their corresponding feelings in my memory—all the images—are the cause of my pain.

So I see that retaining all of these images—the wedding, the anniversaries, my husband bringing me flowers year after year—allows me to believe that he loves me and gives me a feeling of security. His simple forgetfulness is only a stimulus for my insecurities to surface. My hurt lies in the bursting of the bubble of my images of security.

> ❀ *This example may seem inconsequential to you in comparison with all the more serious suffering in the world. But because this sort of thing occurs so often and has become important to so many, it serves here to emphasize the general pettiness of image-making. We are interested in the total awareness of our functioning.*

We see others as well as ourselves according to past experiences, do we not? Even if that past was a minute ago. Thought-memory functions in images, and it is from these that our behavior ensues. In the example above, I have an image of my husband and his love, which I equate with bringing flowers. Furthermore, I have an image of myself secure and content.

If, at this point, the observation is total, objective, without preference, I may see further into myself. I may realize that my self-esteem depends on recognition by others. And that my happiness is fragile and dependent on my husband remembering our wedding date! In other words, I depend on him psychologically for my well-being.

If I keep alert, I may even learn how thought operates:

good feelings depend on the memories of others and their actions toward us. When all goes according to schedule or when it goes the way we think it should, we feel happy and satisfied. We do not recognize that satisfaction depends on memory.

> ✿ *Please note that when things go accord-ing to our expectations, we feel satisfied and we call this feeling happiness or fulfillment! Can you observe if this is so in your life?*

If, purely through observation, we see the *truth* about ourselves, as in this example, the absurdity of feeling upset becomes clear and the hurt vanishes in the moment.

Seeing the *way it is* through this natural process of ob-jectivity, which we are here calling *objective self-observation*, we then experience a sense of well-being and peace of mind. This allows us to experience love. We need to recog-nize the destructiveness in our relationships when the ruling force of our behavior is thought-memory. We need to inquire if there is an intelligent, aware way of living based on a process of the moment and not preempted by memories of the past.

> ✿ *We are pointing to something outside of the mechanical thinking system. Find out about this for yourself. You can do this right now, by investigating your own thought process.*

Coming back to our example, let us look at the cause of the problem by asking, "Was it caused by the husband's attitude or by the wife's emotional reaction?" If we answer yes to either of these, we might go to a friend and talk it over, in order to solve the problem and eliminate our feel-ings of pain. Looking deep into our functioning, perhaps we can see that the emotions are the result of a conflict within ourselves, a clash between *what is* and our established image of *what should be*. So the cause of the pain is *this conflict*, not the factual situation of what is. Being aware of this, we might not wish to alleviate each hurt, as we usually do; instead we may go into the nature of the conflict that such images cause.

While we are attempting to know ourselves, we often delve into the past and try to understand each hurt, as in psychotherapy. But this is a very long process. And even by understanding a thousand hurts we cannot avoid being hurt again, *because the image-making system never stops.* The psychotherapeutic mode of investigation may be appropriate for someone who is experiencing great emotional upheaval or someone who has been severely abused or psychologically injured from childhood. Upon completion, the person could then begin a different kind of process—a journey of direct inquiry.

Responsibility and Blame

Before continuing, we want to be sure that our way of looking is responsible—that is, when we are observing, there is no blame. Let us take another common example to clarify what we mean by *objective observation*. Let's say that someone calls me an idiot and I respond with hurt. I truly believe that if I had not been called that, I would not have suffered. I further believe that I am absolutely right about this. It is the other person's fault: "After all, I was fine until someone called me that name." So says my mind!

> ✿ *Do we not usually act this way? If you wish, you have the opportunity to observe yourself now. Do you feel you have been hurt from childhood and perhaps believe that you can never get rid of those scars?*

In this example I am so busy blaming the other person for my discomfort that I miss the opportunity to see myself and understand my behavior. Note that here the important factor is psychological comparison. There must be one image for *smart* and another for *idiot*. The former I definitely think is me. Perhaps I have often been complimented by my teachers or parents. So there is a conflict between yesterday's compliments and today's insults, and the result is a feeling of being assessed as *less* today than yesterday. For in my computer (the brain) it is good to be smart and bad to be an idiot. My image of myself, then, depends on the opinion, judgment, or evaluation of others. In other words, it depends on conditioning—mine and that of others—and on whatever program may be in the brain.

Such a relationship is like that of one computer to another, one image to another! To look responsibly, which is objective observation, is to look without images, without input from any memories. We may have never really seen ourselves this way. Perhaps all we know of ourselves is imagery!

> ❦ *Please find out. How do you know your-self? To be "at observation" is to be without images. Observe gently.*

Is it possible to live so responsibly—or, perhaps better, "response-ably"—that we always have a total response to every challenge, never place any blame, never have a second thought about our reactions, our hurts? Can we live without resentment, comparison, competition—which implies living totally without images? If so, all our actions would be appropriate, born of the moment, clear of past experiences, and free from images of the past. Our relationships would be quite different; they would be extraordinarily alive and harmonious!

How can we function without the influence of the past? It truly seems impossible to end society's brainwashing process of conditioning us to prejudices, division, images and repetitive patterns of behavior. *How* is a person to live the *now*?

That is a common and plausible question; nevertheless, it may be a trap. If we look for a way, a "how to do it," we will be back in our predicament of functioning within the thought process that teaches and repeats methods. If we store our new behavior in memory, we are back to imagery, back to conflict between "what is" and what "should be." Memory is not the living now; it is the dead past.

Only when we let go of the need for a method or an authority can we experience direct, objective observation of the image-maker, which is oneself.

> ✤ *Can you let go of "how to"? Could you use this book as a stimulus and not as a new method to deal with problems or hurts?*

Through our conditioned thought-memory process we have developed a way of relating to one another that is destroying humanity. Our conditioning is always operating at the very core of our relationships and self-image.

Here we must be careful not to assume, as many do, that there is one way of thinking that is destructive and another way that is constructive. Please let us notice that all the positive thinking in the world has not done away with nuclear threat, starvation, or suffering. I am not belittling thought, trying to change it, renounce it, or silence it, but just looking at it impartially.

In observing closely the way we relate to one another, it may be noted that we human beings use thought-memory in our relationships in the same way that we do in technology. In correcting our deteriorating relationships, we continue using known psychological tools, methods, knowledge borrowed from an expert, instead of spontaneous understanding of ourselves and others in the moment of *now*.

> 🌹 *Please look into your own relationships.*
> *It may be difficult to confront yourself—*
> *it is easier to talk or read about it!*

Discovering Yourself in the Act of Living

Methods such as psychotherapy or psychoanalysis are not detrimental. We are simply pointing to the repetitive modes of teaching psychological doctrines and their unquestioned acceptance—as if they were the final truth about human nature. We are emphasizing the fact that following or becoming fixed on one psychological model or another eventually takes away from *the discovery of oneself in the act of living*.

We have seen in our exploration that we cling to memories of the past and inject these into the present or project them into the future. We see one another according to the way we were treated yesterday. Hanging on to the remembrance of pleasure, we strive for more of the same. Recalling our discomforts or hurts, we try to avoid experiencing those sensations again. The memory of a traumatic experience keeps us in fear, even when there is no longer any danger. After an automobile accident we may have nightmares and wake up as afraid as if the situation were real. We may be extremely cautious or even afraid to drive again. Accepting and remembering compliments of yesterday, we may be upset if we are criticized today. Often children, as well as adults, develop a craving for recognition and end up on a constant emotional teeter-totter from pride to shame. They feel on top of the world when applauded and totally dejected when criticized.

Our way of looking at ourselves psychologically is as

fragmented as humanity itself. Subjects such as fear, self-esteem, and communication (there is a very long list) are usually looked at separately, as if each one has a different root, a different causation, which must be dealt with. Our therapies are as fragmentary as humans themselves!

If we try to analyze each fear, each hurt, or each moment of anger and explain them, we will be forever talking about our problems and never truly *dissolving* them. At best, we can alleviate our pain through learned therapeutic methods, and at times that is all we can do. But even when a person is helped temporarily and sometimes totally, psychotherapy is not a remedy for the world at large. World conflict cannot be resolved as long as people are in conflict within themselves. As long as the individual is in conflict, humanity is in conflict!

> ✿ *Are you directly aware of this? Or do you sit and criticize the world situation without that sense of nonjudgmental responsibility that is compassion? Please find out!*

Without total awareness of the wheel of conditioning, humanity cannot transcend this consciousness of suffering and exist in a state of well-being and harmonious living, which is real living meditation, which is love!

Hidden Pathways of Emotion

Rationality and Emotions

Emotions are a primordial and powerful force in human consciousness. Regardless of all the knowledge available on the subject, there remain many contradictions in our views of emotions and behavior.

For example, being without emotion is viewed as a threat to society, an irrational psychopathological state. Indeed, we fear this state of mind; for a human being in this condition is capable of destroying anything and anyone without a trace of remorse. A psychopathic killer is considered a very dangerous human being. Contrary to this, killing with a reason, as in war, is often rewarded. Persons behaving thus in war are considered normal, in a "rational" state of mind, and not a threat to humanity, in spite of the countless atrocities man has committed against his own species since time immemorial. The implication is that rationality is not devoid of emotions, but that some emotions are under enough control to allow soldiers to carry out the "necessary" killing.

In general, people are proud to be the "rational animals" of this earth and feel themselves to be different from the species that hunt and kill for survival. Thus a psychopathic killer is contemptuously considered no more than an animal. The killing of another human being *with or without* emotions or reasons cannot result from other than a deranged state of mind in humanity. Humankind has come to rationalize and justify such behavior, unaware of this animal nature that remains stuck within the psychophysiological structures.

Being asleep (unaware), we continue to attempt to understand our relationships and emotional states. Regardless of all scientific studies in chemistry and physiology, and psychological theories, we remain in the same survival-of-the-fittest state as humans who lived among the animals in the jungles. Moreover, our ability to reason seems to have contributed to damaging the quality of living, escalating our ability to kill thousands of people all at once.

It would be easy simply to identify with all the goodness in humanity and feel proud of ourselves. This would be totally self-deceptive and hypocritical. We need to see all of what we consider goodness as a fact—no more, no less. Conversely, we need to see all we call animalistic, violent, and hideous as a fact—no more, no less.

> ✿ *Are you willing to confront the duality of humanity? The duality in you? See yourself as a totality without avoiding any perturbing feeling or sensation? Take your time to investigate this issue. Put the book down at this moment if you need to do so. Look neutrally at humanity, compassionately!*

Up to this point in our journey, it has been important for us to look at our rationality. Now we can move to a deeper inquiry into our emotions. It is imperative to explore humanity's emotional functioning directly in ourselves, as individual parts of the whole. Thus we can experience the truth of human nature in its totality.

A Different Approach to Fear

The object of our inquiry in this section is fear, primarily because of its connection to the other emotions, but also for its primitivism, its persistence, and its consequences in humanity.

Our approach to fear is not from an established point of view or from that of a psychological discipline. We want to look at this emotion directly in ourselves, using knowledge as a stimulus rather than an explanation of what we experience. In this manner we can be cognizant of what fear is, and we can go beyond an intellectual understanding. We further intend to expand our awareness beyond that of the desire for emotional relief.

Therapeutic techniques have been designed primarily to discharge (express or release) and to understand emotions that have been repressed or consciously suppressed. Our investigation will not be psychotherapeutic in nature, but rather a direct, objective observation of ourselves, without judgment or evaluation. For this we will explore the conditioning that forms our present mental structure as well as our functioning as members of the human species.

Through the years our conditioning has encompassed opinions, prejudices, beliefs, and evaluations that remain as mental-attitudinal sets. For example, we are cognizant but *not deeply aware* of the great influence of seemingly innocuous phrases we learn and pass on from generation to generation.

Some of the emotional views of fear are that it is a paralyzing emotion, it is necessary for survival, it is something to get rid of or at least something to conquer.

These attitudinal sets constitute our psychological condition. The investigation will take us to an exploration of our general way of thinking (attitudes) and a deeper look into the meaning of emotions in general.

> ✿ *If there are any of these views in your*
> *mind, an examination of them may be*
> *very important. Remember that you are*
> *responsible for your own personal views*
> *or biases. Thus you are encouraged to*
> *look within yourself, compassionately.*

The Nature of Emotion

Emotions are a conscious psychosomatic activity we experience directly rather than an unconscious automatic activity like digestion, of which we cannot be directly cognizant, since it is under the control of the autonomic nervous system. Emotions involve the autonomic and central nervous systems as well as the cerebral cortex, which is the basis of our consciousness. It can be argued here that we experience emotions and feelings when we are asleep. In the dream state, the organism is active; the brain as well as many other organs are involved. Research on sleep has proved that human organisms react with physiological symptoms such as perspiration and rapid heartbeat during the dreaming stage, which is also characterized by rapid eye movements. Some of these body reactions do not differ from those we experience during emotional states of waking consciousness. From these data and from witnesses who tell us how we fidget, cry, or talk during sleep, we have concluded that we experience emotions while we are in an unconscious state.

However, it is only upon awakening (cognitive state) that we can *feel* the emotion; or we may feel it later, when we remember the dream. If upon awakening there is no memory of any dream, we

1. may not have dreamed;
2. may not be experiencing emotions;
3. may be experiencing physical discomfortbut not feeling any particular emotion such as fear, anger, happiness; or
4. may not be experiencing any particular sensations and still be feeling an emotion.

Regardless of how we awaken, we are aware of emoting only during waking consciousness, for in a state of unconsciousness we are oblivious to the body sensations and the emotions. We cannot determine whether we experienced emotions in our sleep without the memories of a dream, a sensation upon awakening, or the observations of someone else.

During our investigation, the above discussion of emotions in the dream state will serve as clarification of our understanding of unconscious emotions.

Whether we are emotional or not during sleep need not concern us. That is a subject for scientific research. Many researchers are now involved in investigations of the dream state, and there are different opinions about the subject. We are inquiring directly into ourselves without the use of witnesses, as in sleep labs, to tell us what is happening to us.

We will address the processes involved in the total experience of emotions, beginning with the concept of the word as defined by the dictionary. Then we will move on to an observation of emotion as a process in ourselves. Webster defines emotion as: 1. strong feeling; excitement; the state or capability of having the feelings aroused to the point of awareness; 2. complex reactions with both physical and mental manifestations such as love, hate, fear, anger, etc.

To be more comprehensive in our inquiry, we want to consider the dictionary definition of the word feeling as well. Webster defines feeling as: 1. sense of touch; 2. the power or faculty of experiencing physical sensation; 3. an awareness; consciousness; sensation; 4. an emotion; 5. an opinion or sentiment.

Emotion, according to the dictionary description, implies an intense feeling with physical as well as mental manifestations. Feeling, according to Webster, "when unqualified in context, refers to *any of the subjective* reactions, pleasurable or unpleasurable, that one may have to a situation, and usually connotes an absence of reasoning."

> ❦ *Look at your experience. Is fear an emotion or a feeling? Both are similar aspects of inner activity.*

We see that emotions encompass the psychic mind function of the human organism from its inception. Through psychology we have learned that emotions can be unconscious as well as conscious; this seems to be our interpretation or belief. For a more thorough understanding of our own experience of emotions, we may contend that *emotions or feelings are felt only in a state of waking consciouness.*

Of course, the general concept of emotions stands in contradiction to this statement. We have traditionally believed that we accumulate repressed emotions—that is, they become buried in the unconscious and eventually they erupt, coming through to our consciousness, causing emotional imbalance.

The dictionary says that emotions are a "state or capability of having feelings aroused to the point of awareness." According to this definition, emotions or feelings can be unconscious as well as conscious. However, emotions do not imply a latent energy; rather they are an *activity* in the organism.

The notion of unconscious emotions, rather than being erroneous, is simply a cause for confusion, because it closes the door to total awareness by fostering a dualistic notion of consciousness. What is unconscious is *not* the emotion, but the *memory of the content* of a past emotional experience or feeling. Thus the emotion per se is not repressed, but rather the memory of the incident (the image) is what is retained. Furthermore, associated with this is the memory of the *intensity* of feeling, also maintained as memory. This is an important factor in our understanding of emotions. It is *not* the energy that is generated in the moment of the emotion that is repressed and therefore dammed up. It is more like the movement of energy generated during a storm. Thunder is not an energy held in the clouds as they move, but rather the *result* of atmospheric conditions; nor is the wind held back in the storm clouds, but rather conditions will cause the wind to start up and subside.

Stimulus and Suppression of Emotions

Similarly, emotions are the result of specific conditions in the organism; they begin when a stimulus is presented either from the outside or from the inside (memories or chemical and physiological imbalances), and then they subside.

> ✿ *Look for yourself and see if you can re-press energy per se. Observe what happens to you when fear comes up. Is that an old energy? Or is the energy a movement, an activity of the organism at the moment?*

The content of the so-called suppressed or repressed emotion consists of the memory of incidents and the intensity of associated feelings at the time. When the person forgets (represses) an event associated with feelings of fear, then upon retrieval or upon some stimulus that brings about even *parts* of the image or memory of feelings associated with the incident, he or she may experience fear as in the past. You have heard people say that they relived an incident when they recalled some past experience. The process of psychotherapy aims at the remembrance and retrieval of images and at the discharge of the intense feelings associated with them. These memories, once retrieved and experienced, supposedly will not bother the individual again.

However, emotional abreaction[1] of memories can occur over and over again, and this indeed happens. It is especially repetitive in certain cases when there is a secondary or residual gain in remembering and discharging—for example, the show of sympathy by others when a person cries. It is understandable how this can occur, since it is in the nature of our functioning to retain images and the memory of the intensity of feelings. Even after discharging by recall, we can keep the memories and repeat the process of discharge until it becomes automatic behavior.

Sometimes a person seems to be a professional "discharger" of emotions. Each time there is a discharge of emotion—crying or a burst of anger, for example—the person feels better, thinking the situation has been resolved. This may become a repetitive pattern, usually associated with some sort of reward, such as sympathy; thus the person is ever ready for the next upheaval, discharge, and reward.

A young lady who had been labeled schizophrenic was

---

[1] The expression and emotional discharge of unconscious material; a repessed idea or emotion, for example, by verbalization, especially in the presence of a therapist.

assigned to me as a patient at a clinic in Los Angeles. The case was considered almost impossible. The patient had to be able to leave the clinic within eight weeks—in other words, she had to be functioning well enough to keep from being hospitalized or kept in the clinic.

In the first interview she cried intensely about her problems.

I asked her, "Why do you cry?"

She responded, "Because the psychiatrists tell me it is good for me; I have to release my emotions."

"Does it help?" I inquired.

"No," she responded, "but it is good for me. I am always encouraged to release my emotions by crying."

"Yes, but does it help you?" I insisted.

"No," she said, "I am sick and tired of crying, and I am still afraid."

"Well, why don't you stop crying?" I suggested.

"But I am told I need to do it!" she said.

"But you just told me that it doesn't help. Why don't you use your intelligence instead?" was my firm question.

She stopped crying. Eight weeks later she had a job; she was the talk of the clinic staff.

The brain can easily be conditioned to emote, and this conditioning is reinforced by the encouragement to discharge or express emotions. This is encouraged because to hold back, which is to suppress or repress, may have an injurious result in the organism. This seems to happen more readily in some individuals. Many ulcers are said to be caused by constant unreleased emotional tension. Any continuous tense state will, of course, eventually damage the body. So the general advice of medical and psychological professionals has been to express and discharge emotions.

Until recently, techniques such as meditation had been overlooked as relaxation processes to help calm the emotional states. Actually, meditation has the same effect as the release of emotions. Both relax the organism. The fact is that we are conditioned not *to relax* but *to discharge*.

One wonders if we have become a generation of "dischargers." Our present youth, having been conditioned to self-expression, certainly have followed instructions well! This is obvious not only in their emotions, but also in their music, dress, and general behavior, one may add, to the chagrin of many. Unfortunately, this is not recognized as simply conditioning.

> ✿ *Please observe yourself in the light of emotions. What happens to you when you are emotional? Are you conditioned to express?*

If we are *conditioned* to express or discharge emotions, we may never have a chance to go beyond this state unless we as individuals are willing to experience for ourselves, without reasons or explanations, our own emotional functioning. This means we must experience the generated energy of the emotions without expressing or trying to change the feelings, sensations, and thoughts that accompany this psychological state.

Observation versus Expression

Our total awareness of present human functioning will bring us to the awareness of the need for a radical change in humanity. This change may not be a very easy thing to accomplish. Nevertheless, it is challenging to experience emotions in their totality. To feel every sensation and experience every thought and every nuance in the body during an emotional moment is an extraordinary occurrence. In order for this experience to be complete, there can be no desire for things to be different than they are in that very instant, and one cannot have a justification or reason for the feelings. This is a state of complete alertness. The person is *at observation*; there is *witnessing* of:

1. thought as thought without belief in the content;
2. sensations as sensations without classifying them as good or bad;
3. the wish to end or continue the emotions without expressing or wallowing in them.

It is as if everything is still except the energy movement of sensations, thought and feeling. The body does not act out the inner disturbance; there is no expression, suppression, judgment or evaluation. Emotions such as anger and fear may feel unbearable, since there is no conditioned response to alleviate them. However, once the extremely acute moment of sensation and feeling is reached, a great burst of energy envelops the whole being like a peaceful white cloud. This is a great leap in consciousness; it is like crossing an ocean in an instant and finding the other shore to be something extraordinary, something one has never experienced before.

> 🌹 *Have you ever challenged yourself to experience your emotions **totally**, without any movement other than that of the inner emotional energy itself?*

This process is not recommended for people who are emotionally unbalanced or incapable of remaining still without repressing their emotions.

> 🌹 *You are responsible for deciding if this process is for you. Be gentle! Perhaps you can start by asking what is anger or fear in moments when you are not too upset.*

When we observe ourselves reacting, we are also witnessing humanity's modus operandi. A total awareness of present human functioning will bring us to the awareness of the need for a radical change in mankind.

Fear and "I"

Earlier we mentioned phrases that conceal attitudes—mental sets that are learned and then passed on from generation to generation. Let us see if we can find clues to a deeper understanding of our functioning in the area of emotions.

Let's take this example: "Fear is paralyzing." This particular view or mental set expresses the psychophysiological action of this emotion. Whether the person freezes, attacks, or takes flight, it is obvious that the whole body reacts. We are definitely aware of how we feel while experiencing fear, regardless of how confused our thought process may be at that moment. Quite often we feel that our bodies do not want to move, even though we want to run; at other times we want to speak or scream, but we cannot utter a sound.

Such was the case for Betty. Early in childhood she was frightened by a group of children wearing Halloween costumes. She stood there screaming, unable to move. Her father came to rescue her from her predicament. This incident became the *cute story* about Betty among the adults in her family. They referred to her reaction as being *paralyzed with fear*. Betty began to believe that fear was indeed a paralyzing emotion. "I always freeze up when I am in front of people. Fear is so paralyzing!" she complained. "How can I overcome it?"

Like Betty, we talk about fear as something we do not want to have, or something we want to control. It is important to notice that there seems to be a separation between the "me" and the fear.

❦ *Please look at your experience. Isn't*
there an "I" that says, "I do not want to
feel this bad; I do not want to be afraid?"

This separation between "I" and that which is happening in the body does not seem to have been addressed by psychological professionals.

❦ *How do you experience yourself as "I"?*

We want to observe ourselves carefully to see how it is that we mentally experience being "I." What are these emotions that make our bodies uncomfortable and dictate our mode of action, often contrary to our way of thinking or of viewing ourselves? It is this discrepancy or division within ourselves regarding emotions that we want to explore.

❦ *Please remember that we are questioning*
ourselves in order to experience aware-
ness rather than to learn a new concept
to repeat.

The body and mind are one unit. Human beings are particular organizations of atoms gathered into molecules that form organs and a muscular and skeletal structure. We are psychosomatic, meaning that psyche or mind is an aspect or function enfolded in the soma, or body. Furthermore, we are a species that can think and accumulate knowledge. Therefore there is only one entity, having various functions interacting at the same time.

To examine oneself as a unit may still be a dualistic activity, for who is examining? And what is being examined? Perhaps the examination is all we can do at this moment. It is impossible to express anything in words without division, since our language is the product of our thinking function—that intelligence or ability to abstract and formulate symbols in a divided fashion. Thus it is in our own nature to be divisive. Just as we can think, "I am good," so we can think "I am bad," "I am afraid," "I don't want to be afraid," and so forth.

> ✿ *I'd like to ask you not to accept this as an explanation; rather, challenge it! Inquire for yourself!*

When we are trying to get rid of fear, it does not occur to us to ask, "If I don't want to be afraid, *who does?*"

We perceive ourselves to be this split entity, and this division is very real to us. One thought says, "I am afraid." And another says, "I don't want to be afraid." Thus a battle within ourselves ensues, compounding all the discomfort brought about by what we call fear.

We said that there are two elements to emotion: mental and physical. By definition, thought is the mental aspect of emotion, and feeling (sensation) is the body aspect.

Looking at this experience of "I," what is this "me" in a moment of fear?

> ✿ *Please ask yourself this question right now, as though you have never inquired into it before, even if you have.*

Is "me" or "I" the organism that thinks? Is it "I" that feels tension, pain, and all the other sensations that go with fear?

> ✿ *Have you noticed your sensations as something extraneous that you can get rid of?*

The inquiry into this apparent but illusory separation is very necessary. The cognizance of "I" being an illusion has been discussed in many philosophical and religious treatises. However, we do not wish to use someone else's belief in our inquiry. The total experience in awareness of this division that seems so real to us is a *must* if we are to understand deeply our functioning.

Are not "I" and the fear the same, just as mind and body are the same? We previously asked, "Who is examining and what is being examined?"

> ✿ *To ponder on this, my friend, without answering from what you know, but simply remaining with the question, may be difficult. However, it may be very necessary for an experience of living awareness.*

Observing Fear

Suffering from fear, we attempt to placate, resolve, cope, and negate it—all in an effort to control an occurrence that is natural to our organism. The human body functions in such a way that the experience we call fear is simply a normal reaction. The state of fear becomes unhealthy or extreme—a mental disease we call *anxiety neurosis*—when the individual is overwhelmed and no longer is capable of using all the ways he or she *learned* to cope and to control.

We have labeled fear a reaction to a real threat to survival. We believe that because of fear, animals run or fight when threatened, and we seem to believe that humans are also animals that react instinctively in the same manner. The added difficulty for humans is that we have the ability to abstract, to imagine, and through this natural function we can suffer as much, and in the same way, when we imagine a threat as when the danger is real.

We do not seem to be aware of the power of the imagination as a natural function of the organism; quite often we hear someone say to a child or an adult, "Don't worry, it's just your imagination," dismissing the reality of the bodily experience and the suffering of the person at the time. This lack of compassion is simply ignorance or a lack of understanding of ourselves as human beings. Whether we are reacting to the threatening roar of a lion in front of us, or to the memory of a traumatic situation such as an accident, our bodies go through the same chemical reactions. We experience the imagined stimulus as well as the real one in the same painful manner, and the tendency is to avoid pain at all cost.

Because of our conditioning, we have become intolerant of anything that might bring even the slightest discomfort. Our aversion to discomfort seems to grow in direct ratio to our success in achieving comfort. We want pleasure, but not its inevitable counterpart, pain.

The more we believe that it is bad, wrong, or intolerable to feel fear, pain, anger, or other so-called negative emotions, the harder we try to change the very nature of our organism. It seems that human beings, in an attempt to feel secure and comfortable, are increasingly conditioning their bodies to be something other than what they are. It is remarkable that it is our own natural enfolded intelligence that allows all of this to occur.

> ✿ Can you observe all of this within
> yourself?

The fear in humanity has escalated to such extremes that we have surrounded ourselves with imaginary frontiers and very real nuclear weapons to protect ourselves.

> ✿ Can you see the incongruity of human
> beings? Can you see it in yourself?

On the one hand we develop all kinds of methods, techniques, and theories to allay our fears, while on the other hand we create and surround ourselves with weapons of such magnitude that the inhabitants of the earth live with the constant threat of extinction, consciously or unconsciously.

How can we say we don't want to be afraid while continuing to construct machinery and buildings that inevitably will bring some feeling of fear in special situations?

For example, when we hear of a airplane accident, we keep this in memory, and the next time we are in an aircraft the thought and feeling ensue automatically: "What if we crash?" The thought may be conscious and we may call it apprehension or mild concern. Or we may have a physical reaction, such as dizziness, sweaty palms, or butterflies in the stomach, without a particular thought or awareness of any connection to an apprehension about flying (denial).

The sentence "I don't want to be afraid" is really just an attitudinal mental set we learned; it does *not* stop us from being afraid.

❀ *Have you noticed this happening to you? Observe meticulously.*

I have found fear to be the most popular subject for dialogues among participants in the Self-Studies Foundation in the United States and the Latin American countries I have visited. Fear is an ever-perplexing emotion prevailing in humanity. Scientifically, we have done no more than try to explain it or alleviate it with drugs.

Fear:

From Memory to Observation

Is it possible to look at ourselves in the very moment of fear and observe exactly what is happening, without naming the occurrence "fear?"

> ❦ *Have you ever done this? Have you questioned what is actually happening in your organism? Perhaps it is not easy, but it is not impossible!*

We must remember that we have mental sets screaming, "I don't want to be afraid!" or "I hate it when I feel this way!" Therefore, inquiry at the moment of fear is not possible for a mind caught in the double bind of experiencing all kinds of physical reactions and simultaneously desiring to stop them. For some clarity and inquiry to occur, there must be at least a cognizance of our usual way of functioning: in preferences, opinions, and attitudes.

To overcome automatic emotional responses, pilots, astronauts, physicians, and other professionals go through very intense training to accustom themselves to all that happens in the body and still perform appropriately in moments of fear. These professionals literally recondition their responses. We are so adept at conditioning that after several years of repeatedly performing difficult tasks, we become automatic and unemotional in our performance of them, so that emotions do not interfere with our tasks. Most of us have experienced this once we have learned to drive a vehicle comfortably.

It does not seem feasible, however, for us to train ourselves for every situation in life, because it is the unexpected that concerns us. How can we prepare for the unexpected?

Separation of Fear from the "I"

Given our present functioning, our present consciousness, a life free of fear is a rather illusory expectation. This does not mean that it is *impossible* to have a fear-free life, which would be a transformed life. Again, I must emphasize the *need* for transformation of the species. Human transformation is not an impossibility.

> ✤ Observing these things directly, without believing, opens doors to the total awareness of the human process.

An important aspect to observe is the incongruity between mental sets (beliefs) and the actuality of being human (our functioning).

For purposes of further clarification, let us conduct this imaginary dialogue:

Question: When we try to get rid of fear, what are we trying to discard? The body reactions?

Answer: The mental anguish and the body reactions.

Q. Is there an "I" that can control these re-actions? If so, where is "I?" Is "I" in the body?

A. I am more than just the body.

Q. If you feel you are not just your body, then why did you let it produce the fear in the first place? Why did you allow it if you didn't want it?

A. Well, the body controls me.

Q. If your body controls you, where are you in the body that *it* can control you?

A. I am a spiritual entity.

Q. Do spirits talk and think?

A. Yes, in the body they do.

Q. Then is it your spirit that is uncomfortable or your body that is uncomfortable?

A. No, my spirit is okay, but my body is not.

Q. Then if your spirit is okay and that spirit is "you," why are you complaining about fear? "You" are okay!

While this dialogue may seem amusing here, it was taken from hundreds of serious talks I have had with people.

Separation of body-mind or body-spirit is very real to us, regardless of how much we have learned about one-ness. We have this ancient mental set that comes through our functioning. If we were to replace the word "spirit" with "mind" in the above dialogue, the separation of "I" would remain, either as body controlling mind or vice versa. Sometimes we may even see a triple division. The dialogue may sound something like this:

> **Participant.** I am often afraid, but I cannot do anything about it. My mind just won't stop!
>
> **Questioner.** Where do you feel afraid? Where?
>
> **P.** In my mind (pointing to head).
>
> **Q.** How do you know it's there?
>
> **P.** Because I feel it; I get headaches.
>
> **Q.** Then your body feels it?
>
> **P.** Yes . . .well, my legs shake, my heart pounds. . . .
>
> **Q.** So who is afraid, you or your body?
>
> **P.** My mind and body all together, I guess. But I don't want to be afraid.
>
> **Q.** But your mind does?
>
> **P.** Yes. I tell it to stop but it won't (laughingly).
>
> **Q.** So your mind controls your body?
>
> **P.** Oh, definitely!
>
> **Q.** Now, if your *mind* controls your *body*, where are "you" all this time?
>
> **P.** Ah?
>
> **Q.** Well, are you your mind or your body or something separate from what is going on? Spirit? Soul? What?
>
> **P.** I am *me*. . . . but I don't want to be afraid.
>
> **Q.** Yes, I understand; but where are you while all this is going on? In your mind? In your body? You seem to have no control over mind or body; are you spirit?
>
> **P.** Well . . . I do not know what I am, but I know I don't want to be afraid.

This same dialogue is repeated over and over again. We are speaking of fear, but we could substitute any other unwanted emotion, such as anger. Furthermore, we could use any addiction such as smoking or overeating and have the same kind of conversation. For example:

> **Questioner:** Are you overweight?
> **Answer:** Yes, it's terrible!
> **Q.** Do you want to be fat?
> **A.** No, I don't want to be fat. I just can't help it.
> **Q.** If you do not want to be fat, who does?
> **A.** Not me, I don't want to be fat!
> **Q.** Who is eating all the food that puts on weight?
> **A.** I am, but I don't want to be fat.
> **Q.** Do you want to eat all you eat, even when you do not need it, and not get fat? Good luck! So, who wants to get fat? Is this your body? (and so on).

We truly live unaware!

Emotions have not been examined as part of the process of the divisionary thinking or the fragmentary functioning of human beings. Perhaps it is time to begin such an examination.

The challenge here is to see that there is no separation between "I" and fear. This "seeing" cannot be a simple logical conclusion or an intellectual agreement; it must be an experiential event that could bring a shift within the function of the human organism.

It is not my intention to explain how the thinking process divides or organizes ideas into images, finally allowing us to believe that "I" is an entity inside the body (for some people a spirit or soul); nor do I intend to explain how it is that this entity feels it is a victim of its own mind. The idea of separation between body, mind, and spirit has been strongly inculcated into our brains for thousands of years. Our *way of thinking* is also thousands of years old and immensely strong. It is important for each of us to take responsibility for exploring human functioning by ourselves, in the very act of living.

> ✿ *Please observe how you experience what we call fear. Is it a sensation, a thought, an energy? Is it something foreign to you? Or is it born out of your way of functioning? If so, are you totally responsible for the way you feel, the way you are?*

At this point it would be very easy to discuss ways of looking at ourselves through methods or philosophies. A word of caution is needed. Remember, the purpose of this book is to encourage you to use your own wisdom, without comparing or referring to some discipline or fixed point of view.

Furthermore, this book does not propose that you *believe* in "being solely responsible for yourself"; if this is a truth, not a belief, there will be a natural experience of what total responsibility is.

Thinking responsibility is not necessarily the *living action* of being totally responsible.

> ✿ *I must admit to you that as I read over these pages, I see over and over again how little we know ourselves directly, without someone else's explanation. Do you experience this? Through your own investigation you will come to a new experience of yourself.*

Fear: a Reality?

Someone has said that fear is "false evidence assumed real." For example, if there is a long heavy rope coiled on the ground, we may assume it to be a snake and be terrified. Or we may see a shadow cast on a wall that looks like a human body and assume it to be an assailant, and we may panic. The evidence here, as interpreted by the brain, is false.

Obviously, in the above examples the "reality" is an illusion of the brain resulting from misinterpretation. If we change our example of evidence to a real snake or a lion, the fear would be a reaction to true evidence; the interpretation would not be an assumption.

This view is generally accepted in our present way of thinking. Fear, from this point of view, is not always "false evidence assumed real." Fear may be a reaction to true evidence.

Are there real fears and unreal fears? Are there two kinds of fears? Or is fear always unreal or always real?

> ❦ *Observe your own reactions of fear. Do you react to false evidence in the same way that you react to factual evidence? What happens in your organism? Take time to observe.*

We cannot deny the physical activity of the body. Regardless of the stimulus, our emotions—whether anger, fear, hate, or love—are very real to us, and some are overwhelming.

The evidence or stimulus has little to do with *how* we react. Two people looking at the same shadow may react very differently. Reactions come automatically, depending on the content of memory, the conditioning, and the attitudinal sets.

Fear, *as a reaction* in the organism, is *always a fact.*

We need to examine our way of perceiving and interpreting stimuli; the difficulty lies in how we experience and interpret through the network of mental structures.

Are fearful reactions dependent on the stimulus (outer

evidence) or are they always produced by inner stimuli (memories)? Is there fear without memory of previous experience, some learned forewarning, some knowledge? Or does the brain, through genetic inheritance, already have memories of all past experiences of humanity (reincarnation, for example, and memories of previous lives) as some beliefs or philosophies claim?

> ✿ *Do you have knowledge (information from teachers) about reincarnation or previous lives? Do you really know? Gently look, allowing any insight to come to you from the deepest inner space of your being. It is all there!*

Observing animals in the savanna is a most impressive and interesting experience. Animals kill to survive. Deer and zebras, as well as other animals, run for their lives at the sight of predators. The awesome behavior in some of these animals is their stance (attentively standing very still) while lions are nearby, walking toward a water hole. The fact that they may have memories of lions chasing for a kill does not seem to bring about any behavior we would call fearful. Deer and zebras run only when a lion is on a hunt; this means they are interpreting the evidence correctly. Unlike humans, they seem to stay just naturally with the facts.

> ✿ *What can you learn about your own functioning from animals and from nature?*

From Instinct to Memory

Our ability to abstract and retain in memory our past experiences has given us a great deal of trouble and caused much pathological behavior. We have been dealing with emotion as something we must control. Psychological and medical techniques for controlling emotions have been ineffective in the long run for human beings. We are still emotional, irrational, territorial, and warlike creatures, fighting for our survival.

> 🌹 *Even if this does not apply to you directly, please look at the general attitude in humanity. You are observing for all other human beings in the world.*

Survival is a powerful drive in animals and in humans; at least we have interpreted it this way. However, there seems to be a great difference in kind between the survival drives of animals and those of human beings. Carnivorous animals kill as necessary for survival, maintaining balance among the various species of nature. Conversely, humans kill beyond mere survival needs, upsetting nature's balance.

In the field of reproduction, for example, the aquatic species, particularly those that are prey to larger fish, reproduce in appropriate ratio to the need for survival, maintaining balance in the oceans. Human beings, however, in spite of superior intelligence and abilities, procreate without concern for balance, causing famine and intense suffering.

The outstanding difference in the survival behavior of human beings and that of other animals seems to be that the human's survival is based upon personal, self-centered interest, rather than upon survival of the species as a whole. Pollution is only one result of desire for personal survival in a *particular* way. "Two cars in every garage" is a wonderful convenience for which we are paying dearly in our ecological environment.

Is fear connected to survival in the brain in such a way that we face possible extinction because of our self-centeredness? Is the automatic reaction we call fear the result of a gross misinterpretation by a very complex, highly evolved brain? Have the higher functions of the cortex amplified and distorted the natural drive for survival? Has structured thought, per se, brought the species to a point of no return?

Macabre as this may sound, an overall look at the human predicament, as stated in earlier chapters, seems to affirm this possibility. Careful observation brings us to the emphasis of this book: the imperative need for the transformation of humanity. Let me emphasize that I do not mean a personal, selfish *change* for individual development, but rather *the transformation of the species* for the sake of its own survival and for balance on the planet. For us to experience our true humanness, there must be a transubstantiation in consciousness at the level of soma.

> ❦ *Again, these words are to be used as investigative tools, not as a philosophy to be adopted. If you are inquiring deeply into the consciousness of humanity, you are already in a different dimension of consciousness.*

Education in Labeling Emotions

To our conventional and qualifying way of thinking, there are different kinds and gradations of fear. Challenging this belief may bring us to the realization that fear is simply a label for a particular automatic occurrence in the organism. We may see that such labels serve to distinguish between different occurrences; each of these is a particular automatic emotional activity composed of a set or combination of sensations, thought patterns, and chemical activity associated with specific kinds of behavior. Thus we identify each emotion—anger, hate, love, and so forth.

Observing very young children, we see how, from a very tender age, we are taught to label these emotions. For example, at age three Liza had a tantrum because her mother did not allow her to watch television past her bedtime. Liza sat on the couch with a displeased look on her face, an attitude often displayed by her mother. "Stop pouting" was the reprimand. Liza stood up, threw her doll on the floor and said, "I'm mad! I don't want to go to bed!" and began to cry. Children readily learn to imitate others and to identify their feelings according to the education from their parents.

All emotions are different combinations of the same ingredients involving the whole organism. Through abstraction and language we have learned to qualify and classify, judge and evaluate, and label these combinations of thought patterns, sensations, and chemistry changes. Furthermore, we have constructed beliefs based on our concepts and qualifications.

> ✿ Can you look at emotions in yourself as an occurrence, without labeling, judging, or evaluating them?

We have learned to recognize one set of reactions, among the hundreds of occurrences in the body, as fear.

Little Liza learned very early in her life what fear was. She was petting her cat one day when suddenly another cat appeared on the scene. Unfortunately her cat reacted by hissing, arching its back, and clawing. Liza began crying and ran to her mother.

"It's all right, honey. Don't be afraid. Cats like to fight with one another. Don't be afraid; it won't hurt you." After the intruding cat was removed, the mother brought Liza's pet to her. Liza was reluctant to touch her cat and drew back from it. "Don't be afraid. It won't hurt you anymore," her mother insisted.

Whatever was going on in Liza's body-mind at that moment was now forever to be associated with the word "fear." When this kind of incident is repeated hundreds of times we are conditioned to the experience we label *fear*.

When we speak of fear, our listener knows what we are talking about; everybody knows what fear is! Labels are useful tools for communication. But are they needed in order to go through the experience of a particular emotional occurrence?

Going through an emotion, feeling it without labeling it, without outwardly expressing it, without resisting it, and without stopping the inner activity, will cause the emotion to die. This involves *experiencing the emotion thoroughly within ourselves to its very peak*.

Like flowers, emotions begin to unfold until they are in full bloom, involving the entire being; and just at the peak of maturity, they begin their descent in the process of life itself. Emotions, like flowers, wither on their own, leaving the human body with a sense of completion, freedom, and well-being.

Just as the flower does not need knowledge of its blooming-dying process, no one needs to teach us how to experience going through emotions without labeling, judging, or evaluating them—we do not need to learn how to live. Emotions are part of life as a human being. Our own discovery of natural functioning brings us to a new way of experiencing emotions without trying to suppress, repress, change, or express them.

> ✿ *To investigate and experiment with emotions in this manner is your challenge. Go slowly, be very gentle, attentive, and kind in your experimentation.*

Taking the approach that fear is a particular set or combination of sensations, thought patterns, and attitudes, we see that we do not suffer different *kinds* of fears. This brings simplicity and clarity to the investigation of oneself. It has a great advantage over techniques that investigate each individual fear. Thus it is possible to experience oneself—be totally aware—in the act of life itself, without an explanation of each occurrence of emotion.

Fear of Death: Instinct, Fantasy, or Aberration?

If all there is is fear, not different kinds of fear, the question arises: Is there a predisposition in each of us to experience this emotion? In other words, is fear instinctive, a ready engram to react in a certain way, inherited through the genes? Is fear based on our natural instinct for survival?

> ✿ *We are not looking for answers from our belief systems or from psychological theories. Have you asked yourself these questions anew?*

We experience fear when there is some threat to the organism. It is logical to assume that this is our drive for survival. We do not want to perish. To what extent is death associated with our automatic fearful reactions? Are animals afraid to die while running from dangerous predators? Or is this fear found exclusively in the thought process of human beings? Is fear of death another complex cortical generalization or aberration in the human brain?

> ✿ *Do you see yourself as just being afraid, or as having different kinds of fears? Do you qualify or classify your fears? Or are they just an experience in the organism?*

Our earlier example of the lion and the deer may cast some light on our pondering. When the lion is not on the hunt, the deer does not run for survival, even though a predator is very near. The memory of the possibility of death does not seem to be an issue for the animal, as it is in the human brain.

We are certainly influenced in our reactions and behavior by the thought, the sight, or the possibility of death. The brain is readily conditioned through generalizations, aberrations, beliefs, and knowledge of possibilities. Thus we move about without much awareness. Let us consider each of these conditioning factors in detail.

Generalization means to make or treat as general, or universal; from objects or ideas into classes.

One of the special capabilities of our minds is the ability to generalize. This means that we can extend the meanings of something, through association, to a multiplicity of things to reach *a general conclusion*. For example, our little friend Liza was eventually severely bitten by her cat, establishing a fear of cats in her brain. She began to have nightmares about cats and other animals. Each time she awakened, her mother reaffirmed that everything was going to be all right. "Don't be afraid." By the age of five, Liza had developed a fear of fur garments and of blond adult people. She became withdrawn at the sight of furry objects or very light-haired persons. These objects and people had become associated with being bitten by her cat. Furry clothing reminded her of cat's hair; blond hair reminded her of the other child sitting with her when she was bitten by her cat. Fur and blond hair became stimuli for fear.

The brain generalizes by associating, as in a chain reaction, details of the original trauma or even minor incidents. In Liza's case, her associations were:

cats - fur - blond hair $\Rightarrow$ pain.

Generalization is a normal function of the brain which *can* become pathological.

Aberration, according to the dictionary, means 1. deviation from right, customary, prescribed or neutral course or condition; wandering; error; 2. partial mental derangement.

We have the ability to fantasize, to create images and store them in our memory banks. Through memory, we can fantasize endless stories, experiences and hallucinations, the latter being inner images projected outward. When a fantasy is projected outward and believed to be true, we view it as a hallucination or a pathological state—*except* when the fantasy falls within the accepted speculative framework of society. In this instance it is not considered pathological; it may be accepted as a vision of the future, such as space colonization or a Star Wars defense system, or a "God-given" vision, like those of Joan of Arc.

We may contend that fantasies are aberrations in the sense of deviation from *what is*. Let me elucidate my proposal: In the brain, a memory is just as much an image as something perceived from outside. Thus, in regard to images, the brain does not differentiate between what is happening now and the memories of what has been learned. We may say that any thinking outside of *what is* in the moment of life itself, is fantasy.

According to this statement, we classify fantasies:

1. as *what is*, and justify them. For example, we view a "God-given" vision as *what is* in our religious beliefs. We follow visions of the future, such as Star Wars, believing them to be real now; we carry out research in the present on weapons of the future;
2. as useless, as when we daydream about winning the lottery without playing it;
3. as pathological, as when a person sees things that are not there (hallucinations).

Some of our fantasies may actually be aberrations, and we may be unaware of this.

Having looked at generalization and fantasy as aberration, we may take a deeper look into our concepts of death. Is there a direct connection between fear, survival, and death as a result of this ability of the brain to generalize, fantasize, and make images? Could belief be involved?

Belief the dictionary defines as: probable knowledge; mental conviction; acceptance of something as true or actual. Fear of and fascination with death are persistent in the minds of many. Some people even read the obituary page of the newspaper every day. Often, after the death of someone, particularly a loved one, children as well as adults have nightmares and macabre fantasies. These persist in the memory bank, sometimes for a long time, causing much suffering. Stories and beliefs about death passed on through generations have contributed to a conditioned fear response. Thus, death is not a simple fact of life to us, but rather an event much fantasized about and feared.

In spite of the inevitability of death, we think of it as an opposite to life, an intrinsic evil to be avoided at all costs. The idea of life-death as a natural cycle is accepted by the intellect as a soothing concept; in actuality, however, death is detested and resisted. We are sad when someone dies and happy at the birth of a child, regardless of the fact that both events are normal aspects of the life cycle. In some cultures, people are conditioned to rejoice when someone dies, but the fear of death remains.

Do you fear death? What have you learned about death?

Because of our desire for survival we have adopted endless beliefs about the beyond, about what happens to us when we pass on. Thus we may believe in karma, reincarnation, punishment for our sins, and so forth. The knowledge we acquire through religious and philosophical beliefs gives rise to an emotional and intellectual understanding of death. It instills fears as well—for example, the fear of going to hell. The gruesome representations of death in the movies and on television are more than sufficient to trigger survival mechanisms and fear in a brain that is ever generalizing and fantasizing. Thus fear is continually inculcated through conditioning without our even being aware of this persistent brainwashing.

Concepts of death have tremendous influence on people's behavior. In our civilization many industries, such as health services, are developed for the sake of human survival. We seem to be a death-fearing civilization. It could be argued that appreciation for life rather than fear of death has brought about such massive life-supporting industries. But that is debatable! If humans really had such a great appreciation for life, would they pollute the planet and continue building nuclear weapons?

> ❦ *Please look into this slowly. There is no*
> *intention here to persuade you one way*
> *or another or to give you a new belief.*

Given the mind's capacity to generalize, our natural survival instinct may have degenerated into a more conceptualized fear of not surviving. This is evident in view of the many national boundaries, the abundance of nuclear weapons, and all the devices we have invented to protect ourselves from attack, disease, and other threats.

We have developed a taste for *things:* we adore cars, boats, furs, jewelry, and money in the bank for the future. Survival seems to depend on having many *things*. Through generalization, the possibility of losing them causes fear.

In order to protect all of what we think we need to survive these days, we have invented devices such as burglar alarms, locks, and bars for windows. In many cities the need for protection is so great that almost all the houses in some metropolitan areas have bars on their windows and doors. In San Juan, Puerto Rico, beautiful elaborate ironwork adorns the facades of houses. The aesthetics conceal the owners' fear of losing their possessions. This is evident not only in San Juan but in other cities throughout the world.

Divorces sometimes become fierce courtroom battles when the main issue is fear of losing possessions. When the desire for survival with possessions becomes an aberration, death may be seen as a solution. Suicides are not uncommon after the total loss of a business—surviving without possessions, for some, equals death. The original fear of death is generalized or transferred to fear of not having possessions. Fear of death remains the impetus for action.

We need to become totally aware of life. In this awareness, life-death is simply movement of universal energy.

Summary

In our examination we have taken an overall look at human fear, instead of trying to explain or rationalize personal fears. This approach has yielded the following facts:

1. Fear is an occurrence in the organism, a reaction to inner or outer stimuli.
2. There is essentially only *Fear*, not various kinds of fear.
3. The appearance of a multiplicity of fears comes about through the ability of the mind to generalize and associate.
4. Through generalization, our concepts of death have influenced our natural survival instincts, and from drive for survival we have moved to fear of death.
5. Again through generalization, we have extended mere survival of the body to a specific kind of survival involving a certain life-style.

6. The brain's ability to fantasize facilitates beliefs such as "dreams will come true," or aberrations such as "I cannot live without . . ." These sometimes have tragic consequences.

7. Finally, the desire for power, generalized to the survival of a nation, has resulted in enormous fear of annihilation by nuclear holocaust.

❦ *All of this is a topic for investigation directly into yourself. You will expand on this through your own natural intelligence, your own energy.*

Fear is one of the many emotions we experience as human beings. As we examine, investigate, observe, and study this emotion directly in ourselves, we are seeing all emotions as natural occurrences in human organisms.

The importance of objective observation—without belief, judgment, or evaluation, without an authority telling us how to do it—cannot be overemphasized. We have fallen into various traps of conditioning and we need to awaken and see these traps, *not* to better ourselves or to be superior to any other person, but to contribute to humanity as a whole. We do this when we see, in turn, the contribution of humanity as a whole to the individual, and comprehend the relatedness of all human beings. Then we experience humanness.

To experience our humanness within the realm of universal consciousness is to be humanity itself—one humanity.

Transformation and the Unmanifest

Individual transformation is an ancient topic that has been revived and made popular through the New Age movement. One needs to question the possibility and the potential for such an event in the universe. Can human beings transform themselves through the workings of their minds or through any of the "how-to-transform" courses designed by teachers or gurus? Given the many years of quest for transformation through religious beliefs and practices, and given the state of mind of human beings in general, one cannot help but question whether radical change is possible for individuals through intellectual, scientific, emotional, or ritualistic pursuits.

We do not disallow the possibility of individual transformation; rather, we question the possibility of a total change at the cellular level through our present way of functioning or through our beliefs. Since human beings are totally conditioned through socialization, we must question whether transformation can occur through the conditioned mind or if this is a phenomenon beyond the grasp of the brain.

Perhaps humankind, like the caterpillar becoming the butterfly, must go through contortions and flap the wings of inquiry while going through a transformational process, though the process is initiated by nature itself. Everything is in constant change in the universe, as far as we can observe. However, the human brain wants to maintain the status quo for its own security. It designs beliefs and remains in the circuitry of its own fixed ideas.

Unless we thoroughly question these old circumscribed mind structures, we cannot transcend our present state of consciousness. Our own ability to inquire is the incipient function for a possible change. All we need to do is to follow through with a deep investigation into the nature of our own functioning. Thus, before we talk about transformation, we need to inquire deeply into conditioning and, by examining it carefully, glimpse the Unmanifest beyond it.

We have seen that individual fragmentation, perpetuated through conditioning, is at the core of conflict in the hologram of humanity; the separateness between nations, races, and individuals parallels the separateness between the family and the individual. Therefore fragmentation and the conditioning of humans are worthy of closer investigation, through the process of objective observation without the guidance of an authority.

> ✿ *You are encouraged to continue looking closely, without the use of knowledge (except as a stimulus), observing yourself.*

The Separation of Mind from Body

Regardless of the origin of the human organism on earth, it remains a fact that our physiological structure and our ability to abstract (the mind function) are the basis for our specific development and present way of being. Human beings are a very significant factor in the evolutionary cycle of the earth. Civilization has been made possible by the particular faculties of the human psychosomatic structure. But for certain inherent capabilities resulting from the manifestation of the enfolded intelligence and self-awareness, we would have remained just another animal species roaming the planet. We would still be living in natural jungles instead of concrete ones of our own making.

There is innate intelligence in all living things. Each organism, no matter its size, has a built-in capacity for survival. For example, the amoeba, like any basic cell in the human organism, has all the necessary information, ability, and intelligence to absorb only that which is appropriate for its existence and to reject the unsuitable and the irritating.

One may call this intelligence or ability the *mind function* of living things on the planet. This mind function appears to be part of the universal energy, by virtue of the fact that the earth is part of the universe, which creates its own content. All planets, stars, and other celestial bodies are the content of the universe, as are all the things that inhabit them. It stands to reason, then, that mind, or innate intelligence, is a universal property. Thus in all animate and inanimate structures of the earth there is endogenous mind (intelligence). We perceive this mind function in ourselves as part of our own psychosomatic nature. In an earlier chapter reference was made to the psyche, or mind, aspect—the *subtle manifest*—and the soma, or body aspect—the *obvious manifest*—of human nature.

In the past we believed the mind to be something

separate from the body. Some historians believe that the dualistic view of ourselves began in Greece and was accentuated by Descartes, who emphatically stated that mind was insubstantial (nonmatter), not occupying space, acting through the pineal gland. This deeply embedded way of thinking is reflected in our present language in phrases such as "a sound mind in a healthy body." Dualism became a belief that brought about many misconceptions still reverberating today in the attitudes and teachings of certain established psychological, religious, and philosophical movements. For example, mind control, biofeedback, and other techniques are used to produce changes in the body. The concepts of *will power* and the *power of positive thinking* inadvertently separate mind as a powerful entity. Accounts of out-of-body experiences give a very real impression of an entity separated into mind, soul, and spirit. Indeed, the phrase "mind over matter" carries tremendous significance for many people involved in a diversity of endeavors.

Through psychophysiological research, the theory of relativity, and the postulates of quantum physics, we have changed our intellectual attitude toward the separation of mind and body. However, we may still carry in a collective unconscious-like manner all previous patterns. Thus we remain enslaved by the images of our acquired conditioning. So while being cognizant of the oneness of body-mind, we are still unconsciously caught in our collective memories of beliefs in mind and body or spirit and body.

Phrases such as "we are all one" are easily spoken but seldom lived. Religions and philosophies long proclaiming equality and oneness have not brought about corresponding behavior in the majority of human beings. Our way of living continues to engender and encourage separative behavior.

It is time for us to see that all the words in the world will *not* bring about the kind of change necessary for peace and harmony to humankind. Slogans such as "We are one energy" remain abstractions, unrealized in our daily relationships.

> ✿ *As an experiment, ponder these words*
> *in silence without attempting to find an*
> *explanation.*

Our Learning Potential

A closer look at conditioning, conditionability (readiness to be conditioned), and thought in the human organism is imperative if we are to further confront our own nature.

We have established that there is no essential difference between the fragmentation within the individual and the fragmentation among races and nations. Human conflict exists because of the present mode of functioning of the organism. In previous chapters we also looked at the general state of humanity and the results of the divisionary ways of thinking through thought-memory, possessiveness, comparison, and so forth, and we observed the kind of conditioning that perpetuates separateness, which brings about conflict.

The mechanically repetitive aspect of thought-memory has contributed to the learning process so highly revered by humans. We have proudly used this ability to the utmost, even though some experts on the brain maintain that we are still not utilizing our total potential. Human beings are in awe of their own capacity for knowledge, and continue to promote it.

> ✿ *Is knowledge conditioning? It is up to you to*
> *discover the truth about this. It is up to you*
> *to reflect on these words without believing*
> *or disbelieving what has been written.*

We venerate learning and "higher" knowledge and are oblivious to the insidiousness and morbidity of this reverence. In our own lack of awareness, we have not noticed that our knowledge has brought about a self-centered way of living that makes us capable of mass destruction.

Cognition versus Living Awareness

Our responsibility in this matter is to experience the truth of our own conditioning—the truth as living awareness, *not* as a mental appreciation, an emotional agreement, or an intellectual "Yes, indeed!" (cognition). To be totally *aware* of our conditioning means, in this book, to *live conditioning as a fact*. This occurs when we see it without judgment or evaluation, without trying to evade, change or improve whatever we observe.

The question here is: How does one do this? It would be preposterous to respond with a how-to, after having observed that following someone else's techniques has destroyed our spontaneity and fortified our mechanicalness. It is clear that individuals must discover for themselves the experience of living awareness. However, to clarify further what is *meant* by it, let us first look at cognition, which is also awareness, according to the dictionary.

Cognition is a mental awareness acquired through perception (the senses) or learning by repetition; to know; knowledge.

Cognition is our daily waking life. We are aware through all we learn every day. We begin progressively to cognize from infancy as our mental functions develop. In other words, we begin to acquire knowledge and be more and more conscious of both the world around us and of ourselves.

In contrast to the definition of cognition, *living awareness* or *living action* refers to a spontaneous experience of the whole organism in which every cell is totally involved in the process of *seeing* at that moment; in that instant there is an *alertness to what is* without memory of the past and without an image of the future.

The moment of insight is just this. Anything remembered after that moment is only memory and no longer a living awareness. Thus cognition, knowledge that is memory, is limited. *Living awareness—insight—*has the power of lightning and affects the whole organism intensely. Cognition may be said to be a cumulative process affecting and directing the organism's behavior. This becomes conditioning. *Living awareness* is a spontaneous process deeply affecting and changing the direction of the organism. It is so powerful that it changes attitudes, which are then reflected in people's behavior.

No one can tell you how to have insight, how to experience totally your living action. However, you can discover it as a natural event within your nature, as in the nature of all human beings.

The Persistence of Conditioning

To improve ourselves, find out who we are, or go beyond who we think we are, we have traditionally looked for answers in books, religions, and philosophies. We have explored and researched our societal background and explained our conditioning ad infinitum. We are thoroughly cognizant of the *content* of our programming; but are we totally aware of being conditioned constantly? Are we experiencing our own susceptibility to conditioning, which is referred to in this book as "conditionability?"

Conditioning means: to be affected; influenced; accustomed. *Conditionability* is the *readiness* to be affected; influenced; accustomed.

It stands to reason that if we are conditioned, we must have some readiness, some potential, to allow this to happen. The whole organism must function in a conditionable fashion.

> ✿ *Are you conditioned? Are you condi-*
> *tionable? Observe yourself in this re-*
> *gard, now, directly, without the help of*
> *knowledge, just using your **own** innate*
> *wisdom.*

We need to be alert, for we can easily fall into the trap of creating more conditioning in the very act of reading this book, thus repeating the patterns presented by many of the books, courses, and therapies that aim at *reconditioning*.

> ✿ *Remember, this is a process of investiga-*
> *tion in which this book is the stimulus*
> *and your response is the living action of*
> *the moment.*

Let us repeat: while cognizant of conditioning, humans are *unaware* of their own nature and facility to be conditioned. It would be of no avail to look any further at the already-examined content of conditioning without examining the *core* of the structures or the *readiness* of these organisms to behave according to patterns, habits, and customs.

It is of great importance to see these facts with clarity. However, it would be dangerous to look with judgment, or evaluation deciding whether being conditionable is good or bad. There is a tendency in us to change, modify, ignore, or hide from ourselves that which we dislike; and we tend to emphasize, embellish, or revere that which we approve.

> ✿ *It is very important to see this danger in*
> *yourself. To try to change our natural*
> *ability to be conditioned, or to hide it*
> *from ourselves would be like trying,*

through psychological manipulation, to
change the color of our eyes, or to deny
the fact that we are sensing organisms.

As children, we go through the essential process of ac-culturation (conditioning)—that is, we are affected by, influenced by, and become accustomed to the ways of our society. In order for us to survive on this planet, our bodies must be totally equipped with all the physical structures and functions needed for adaptation. Being an aggregate of cells, the human body accepts or rejects whatever is necessary for the purpose of its own maintenance, through its natural intelligence.

That complex intelligence function (mind) is one of the most important factors in our survival. The brain, the central nervous system, and all the senses are intricately connected in the abstracting functions such as discrimination, comparison, and synthesis. All of these cooperate in the creation of symbology and meaning. Included in this co-operation are emotions, feelings and memory.

These statements of fact are not quotes from scientific findings; they are natural observations. For information about these facts, it is necessary to refer to psycho-physiological studies; a college text might be of interest to some readers.

🌹 *Our purpose here is to look together,*
sensibly—without all the paraphernalia
of scientific work—in order to know
ourselves directly. May we continue to
do this?

We are organisms that are easily affected, influenced, and manipulated by the emotions, attitudes and words of others. This is undeniable. Even the most independent thinker in some way has been influenced by past philosophers, researchers, or religious authorities. The theory of evolution, while a novel view at the time, grew out of Lamarckian geology and the work of several other contemporary thinkers. It was instigated by Darwin, who questioned old philosophical and religious beliefs about creation and who also doubted current biological observations. Even a rebellion against something we have learned—a rebellion that appears to be a new way of thinking—may be directly connected to the old way by acquired knowledge. This may be obvious in view of our own feelings, likes, dislikes, and attitudes, which may seem different from those of our parents or teachers but still remain within what we learned.

> ❦ *Are your feelings, likes, dislikes and attitudes not based on what you have learned? Can you be totally honest about your present attitudes? Are you different from the rest of humanity in having feelings, beliefs, and attitudes? Do you think your feelings and attitudes are unique? Please look, without evaluation.*

Besides being inculcated with beliefs by others, we are also influenced by our circumstances and personal experiences. Do we not keep in memory our past? Does not experience influence our present behavior? We repeat patterns of behavior throughout our lives, and the majority of people on earth carry on traditions and beliefs from generation to generation. This is possible in our species through the computerlike function of the brain, namely memory.

Thought is the principal element of mind function. Memory and thought are two aspects of mind and, at the same time, are the same thing. It is like the two sides of a coin: you cannot separate them. Memory and thought together *are* the coin.

The question is whether or not the mechanisms of memory produce this susceptibility for being influenced, molded, and habituated.

> 🌹 *Would you inquire more deeply into this natural function and its consequences without trying to change it?*

Memory is not peculiar to humankind on this planet, for it is part of the intelligence function of soma—that is, the mind function of all organisms—in a more or less complex fashion. Animal instincts are imprints carried through generations, resulting in repetitive behavior. Plants and cells are programmed to reproduce according to a set pattern. In humans, memory seems to be one of the most important components of the ability to accumulate knowledge, to elaborate, and to create such things as buildings and machines out of natural resources. There has been exhaustive research on memory, but still we have little understanding of it. Controversy exists even in regard to its exact location in the body. One professor at UCLA described his findings by saying, "Memory is wherever you find it." Indeed, some believe that memory resides in the so-called aura of the individual, as well as in the brain. We could speculate that memory is in the very structure of the atom.

> 🌹 *This may be a very interesting thought to ponder or meditate upon.*

Other Conditioning Factors

It would be reductionistic to imply that memory is the only basis of human conditionability. Physical characteristics such as dexterity, upright position, and complex efolded intelligence—namely, the ability to abstract, create symbols and meanings—are also bases for conditionability. Without all these, together with the complex function of memory, we would not enjoy the kind of technological civilization we have, nor would we have cultural traditions. In addition, there are the emotions and the ability to repeatedly respond in specific modes to specific stimuli. The capacity for emotion is definitely a part of this readiness to be affected, influenced, and habituated. It is our sensitivity that allows for reactions. Emotions are also part of our ability to abstract and create meaning.

Our ability to like or dislike is involved in emotional attitudes. We accept or reject, just as the amoeba selects substances for survival and wellness. Unlike this unicellular organism, however, we develop habits according to that which makes us happy or causes us to feel good physically or emotionally, regardless of their appropriateness to our well-being. Emotional likes and dislikes are abstractions that may dictate our way of living—for example, a taste for alcohol or certain foods, or an attachment to a destructive relationship. Emotions become involved in our complicated labeling and interpretations of meaning.

✿ *Please look into these abilities in your-*
   self. How does your mind produce
   meaning? Symbols? Images?

Belief in Past Lives

For the purpose of inquiry into conditionability, let's observe our present beliefs about memory. There seem to be different types of memory, at least in theory. There is the memory of the individual, which encompasses all past events, emotions, beliefs and knowledge; and there is the *past-lives memory*, believed to be stored somewhere in the organism, the brain, or the aura. Recently, past-life experiences have been the subject of psychotherapeutic research. They have also become a new social diversion for some spiritual circles of the New Age. Books and workshops on this topic have been welcomed with enthusiasm.

> ❦ *Perhaps we need to find out for ourselves, rather than accept or reject the belief in a past life. What is your view of past lives?*

Let us follow this intriguing idea. Is there any possibility of past-life memory? As we said earlier, the human organism is psychosomatic in nature. The enfolded intelligence of soma is the subtle, complicated function we call mind or psyche. This is the same enfolded intelligence that exists in all matter, the aggregate of energy of the universe.

If we are energy, and if the components of this energy are in a constant state of change, as has been postulated and proved by scientists to a reasonable certainty, then whatever is engraved in the most minuscule particle of nature is forever in the energy of the universe. This statement in no way asserts the possibility of each individual having had one or many past lives, as many believe. This belongs in the area of *belief* in reincarnation of the organism or the soul.

The point being made here is that *all information is in the energy of the universe, no matter to what particular form of it we are referring*. However, human beings are not in a state of awareness that allows them to do more than postulate or believe; therefore, experiencing the *truth* of this concept remains an act of faith, an *insight* unprovable by science.

The concept that we are unconsciously influenced by collective memories inherited through generations seems quite reasonable. But as a spiritual experience, a psychic phenomenon, or within insight, it is a simple fact.

Memory, whether collective or personal, is a major factor in our readiness to be conditioned. Without it we would not have traditions, beliefs, or culture.

In observing the psychosomatic functioning of human organisms, we see that they are totally equipped to adapt and to be conditioned for survival.

> ✿ *Are you willing to see your own conditioned functioning? Or do you feel you are different? How do you see collective memories? Just be truthful.*

In our state of consciousness we cannot know whether past lives or collective memory are true factors in our conditioning, if we inherit them through our genes, or whether they exist in the human aura. It is up to each of us to explore without belief or disbelief.

The natural ability to experience total awareness is perhaps our grace, our blessing. Within a radical shift of consciousness we can experience ourselves beyond our conditionable nature.

The Need for Transformation

Humankind exists in a limited awareness of changes in consciousness. Through the ages, the knowledge of some changes has fortified a belief that we are evolving in consciousness. Many people believe we have been transformed. Others believe that we will be transformed when some specific event, such as the appearance of a Messiah, occurs. Still others believe they can transform themselves.

Most people do not see any need for a total transformation in humanity. We take for granted that we are an evolving species—*homo sapiens*. A great majority believe we are on a technological spiral in our evolution that will eventually make us superior. Furthermore, there is a prevailing belief in spiritual evolution. According to some, we are beings who are working on our karma, getting better; or we are on an upswing, becoming one people.

The present New Age of spiritualism, by proclaiming the concept of oneness, has perhaps added to the confusion of what awareness truly is. So-called spiritual experiences are not a new phenomenon. These experiences have been occurring for thousands of years. Also, many have claimed to be channels or teachers. All of this has become part of our conditioning.

> ✿ Please look to see what these words
> mean in your experience. What are
> spiritual experiences to you?

Humanity is stuck on a wheel of conditioning, and there is little awareness of this. The general public needs first to be cognizant of this. But as we have said, simple knowledge is not sufficient, for it is only a partial experience. It follows, then, that the masses must experience their own conditioning in a *living awareness*.

While each individual needs to be responsible for *discovering* the truth rather than simply *learning* about it, it is imperative that people at large be aware of their own functioning as being that of humanity itself.

A total experience of the *consequences* of a conditioned mind in this civilization may bring us to a natural realization of the great need for transformation. After a total confrontation with the present state of humankind and a realization that humanity is on the verge of atmospheric and nuclear devastation at its own hands, we can no longer deny the *need for transformation* in consciousness.

The *living awareness of this need* for transformation in human functioning remains an individual experience at the level of being. It cannot be a superficial intellectual or emotional response. When this *need for transformation* is a living action in the masses—when the majority of individuals on this planet experience the *truth* of this need—perhaps then our functioning will be at the point of shifting.

When each of us deals objectively with *what is, as it is,* we are totally responsible. This experience within each of us then becomes a powerful influence in those around us.

What is needed is individual responsibility. This happens *not* by explaining ourselves through given reasons established through knowledge or by repeating the words of this book, or by merely *believing* in the need for a radical change.

> ✿ *Are you willing to be responsible for confronting your conditionability as a living action now? Not expecting a transformation or a desired result, but simply inquiring about the nature of your functioning? Or do you believe you are already transformed and therefore not conditionable? Investigate.*

To be responsible for humanity, to be responsible for the transformation of the species without trying to change ourselves, is to experience the truth of the *needed* transformation.

The transformation of humanity is in nature itself, in the energy that is the universe, in the enfolded intelligence of matter. Our task is just awareness—the living awareness—of the *truth* of this. As the caterpillar is responsible for preparing the cocoon where the mysterious and glorious transformation will take place, so we must do our natural *work*, which is our natural *path*. Our questioning is our preparation.

Unlike the caterpillar, we possess self-awareness and can describe our observations and inquire during this natural process. But like the caterpillar, we do not *do* the transforming. Only through faith in the awesome experience of the universe abiding within ourselves can we surrender to our fate.

You and I are responsible for our experience of this intermittent-eternal process, this pathless path. This, my friends, is life!

Fallacies about Love

Love is a living action. It is "the Unmanifest" experienced in the elusive moment of time. Thus, words can only represent it.

Throughout this book we have been observing the human predicament, our divided functioning, and the results it has brought to this civilization. One can hardly say that there is *love* for one another among members of the human species. Nevertheless, we experience emotions that we call love. We consider certain behavior loving; we also try to teach love, preach it, and enhance the feelings of love through prayer, visualization, and other techniques.

Surely we agree that we experience something we like, something that gives us pleasure and satisfaction, when we feel and express this love, when others express it to us, or when others demonstrate behavior we consider loving. However, this is not a constant *state of being* for people. Like all feelings or emotions, the love we know is temporal, predicated upon our moods and the moods of others, and upon our upbringing.

While there is general agreement as to what love is, the way it is expressed or received varies. In the majority of humans, it is felt as an emotion, with hate seen as its opposite.

In our present consciousness, love is dependent on how we are treated from the moment we are born or, as some maintain, even from the moment of conception. Those unfortunate people who were denied the expression of this emotion cannot function as normal human beings and are often considered aggressive or neurotic. This has been proved through extensive research in psychology, and much has been written on the subject with the appropriate evidence. (A bibliography has been purposely omitted to give the reader an opportunity to choose what kind of knowledge to obtain. Most psychology textbooks provide information on these subjects.)

One person who was denied love in childhood was Martin, a forty-year-old man involved in a child abuse case. Martin was diagnosed as an incurable schizophrenic. His history revealed severe abuse early in his own life. His father, an alcoholic, beat him and sexually abused him. His mother, also an alcoholic, passively and unaffectionately nursed the boy's wounds. Martin grew up in an atmosphere of pleasure-pain and violence. Petrified to tell anyone for fear of the consequences, he withdrew into a morbid fantasy world. Somehow he managed to function sufficiently to maintain himself in his life, but he continued to deteriorate mentally through the years.

At age forty, his abuse of children finally came to the attention of the authorities, and he was committed to an institution; he was treated as a psychopath, incapable of caring for other people. This case is one of the many thousands of examples of the repetition of violent patterns in our society. Our conclusions regarding emotions and behavior are limited to the dichotomy in our way of thinking—love-hate, pleasure-pain.

Since our consciousness is actually fragmentary, the investigations, as well as the proofs, are products of division. Thus one cannot expect psychology to reach any conclusion other than where there is no love there is aggression, fear, or hate—something opposite to love.

Love beyond Emotion

What is being investigated by the social sciences is an emotion, not a state of being.

As long as our relationships are dependent on our emotional state, we cannot enjoy peace among others or within ourselves.

Emotions swing between extremes and are too varied in intensity for the entire human organism to live a harmonious life. A change in this way of functioning is desperately needed if peace is to prevail in the world.

Love is true neutrality; it does not judge or evaluate.

It does not feel good or bad; since it is not mere thought, it does not change into an opposite.

It does not like or dislike.

It does not blame, so it does not need to forgive.

It does not have choices or preferences, opinions or positions.

It does not dictate, is not authoritative.

Love does not differentiate between life and death. It has no expectations other than what is.

Love is not an ideal to venerate; it cannot be known through knowledge or thought.

Love is not words, but the energy of life itself without opposites, without death.

Love is a way of being, experienced by humans and visible only in our actions.

Life and love are synonymous. They are the eternal activity of universal energy without boundaries, movement, or form. Love, being all-encompassing, is the context of all contents of the universe, and thus is infinite. And what is infinite cannot be known within the finite mind. Only in a state of being that is beyond the finite human mind-form can love be the manifest.

Thus love is manifest-unmanifest, form and emptiness. Our minds can express it only in paradox.

Love is all life is and, as such, can only be lived.

Unconditioned Self, Unconditional Love

The Unmanifest is the elusive moment of eternal life; thus it cannot be sought, manipulated, or taught. It can only be experienced as life itself.

In Chapter One we spoke about our psychosomatic nature and its dense and subtle aspects as manifested in all human beings. Also, the Unmanifest was briefly explained as that which gurus and religious teachers refer to as the God Spirit or the Universal Mind.

From time immemorial there have been reports of spiritual and psychic experiences that are considered by many to have come from unmanifested realms. These realms have been called God, heaven, hell, Buddha-nature, and are considered impalpable, unseeable, ethereal states beyond the reach of our normal sensory perception. Experiences of the *presence* of energies, entities, or spirits have been a theme for religious teachings, philosophical beliefs, and superstitions for as long as humans have been on the earth.

The nature of these experiences is as powerful and dominant today as in the past. The experiencer of a *spiritual*, *psychic* or *divine* episode senses a *reality* beyond that of our ordinary linear thinking. The feelings are intense, regardless of the emotion felt, whether fear, delight, or joy. Most often they are difficult to describe. While the content relates to something of the Unmanifest, the reactions in the human body are quite obvious, being an occurrence in the soma, the denser manifest aspect of humans.

Since the experience is psychosomatic, only the *content*, which is the mental aspect, can be said to be unmanifest. The content is the vision or image created in the brain. The associated physical aspects of these images are the electrical impulses in the nervous system and the corresponding bodily sensations. The images—spirits, God, angels, devils, the void, and so on—are of intangible content and impossible to prove as concretely existing through any scientific method.

The materialist or nonbeliever explains the Unmanifest as the product of our imagination. Believers explain it as a religious or a spiritual experience. We have not been able to resolve these opposing views beyond our capacity for belief or disbelief.

It is worthy to note that this is the same dualistic functioning of our present consciousness on the planet. True neutrality, neither believing nor disbelieving, is a state of pure observation. It is a way of being that is enjoyed by the few who dare to not know, who dare to question the nature of humanity's consciousness, who dare to inquire and remain open to truth rather than to intellectual explanations.

True neutrality has no position, no opinions, no preferences or choices, no knowledge, no beliefs. It is a state of *being totally open, vulnerable to all possibilities in the very moment of life itself.* It is this kind of neutrality that is needed for the exploration of these spiritual experiences that are so persistent in humanity.

We will begin by looking at the way in which people have experienced images through altered states of consciousness. Perhaps in the process of this journey, that which is the Unmanifest will be revealed.

Altered States of Consciousness

Visions, ESP (extrasensory perception), premonitions, and foretelling of the future are mental manifestations of a process at the core of humanity's true nature.

Altered states of consciousness are considered to be states that are outside or different from our normal waking consciousness. They are a different reality, special manifestations of a spiritual nature.

The materialistic view of the world, our reality, has a common ground—our agreement. For example, we all see, just as we learned, trees as trees, flowers as flowers, and so on. In an altered state of mind, these things may take a different shape; or forms may be perceived that are not commonly perceived by other people. Thus *Spirit*, or God, is an individual experience that may only be agreed upon through some mental description and explanation.

The experience of the Unmanifest itself (Spirit, God, etc.) is totally subjective. The images and sensations held by the individual experiencer cannot be shared in the same way as an outer object such as a chair, the ocean, or a sunset. These experiences are thought to be manifestations of the supernatural (the Unmanifest) or, in more modern terms, the paranormal.

Until some years ago, science gave little or no attention to paranormal or psychic phenomena. Today, however, many universities have research programs investigating ESP, psychic and near-death experiences, and other altered states of consciousness. This is partly due to a revolution-ary attitude toward mind expansion introduced by Dr. Timothy Leary and others in the late sixties and seventies who advocated the use of psychotropic drugs (drugs that act on the mind), such as lysergic acid diethylamide (LSD).

Seeking spiritual experiences and other drug-induced altered states of consciousness became a popular enter-tainment for a few years, with occasional tragic results, such as suicides and irreversible psychoses. Even some of the pioneering researchers suffered adverse effects, some-time ending tragically. After five years of working with LSD and mescaline, one of the original physicians in Los Angeles doing research in suicides described one of his last experiments with drugs: "I cannot even begin to express the kind of experience I had; all I can say is that the top of my head blew out." He was intrigued and extremely agitated at the same time. Six months later he committed suicide.

There has been great fascination with plant extracts that produce altered states of consciousness. Psychotropic substances are not a new discovery. Ancient cultures used mushrooms and other fungi or plants in their rituals and religious ceremonies. These plants induced powerful visions that were believed to be from the supernatural and were used by the medicine man or head of the tribe to heal, to foretell the future, or to enhance religious rituals.

In recent years, the same fungi and plants or their derivatives, as well as newly discovered mind-altering substances, have been used by many to experiment with different states of consciousness. The intent or motivation for these experiments varies from the personal desire for enlightenment, spiritual experiences, or self-improvement to objective medical research into the understanding and cure of psychoses.

An altered state of mind may be interpreted as evidence of either psychosis or spirituality. Generally, psychiatry views visions as hallucinations, interpreting them as mental aberrations. In contrast, spiritual aspirants never consider a vision an aberration.

In general, people can only believe one or the other, disbelieve both, or assume an "I don't know" attitude. This latter attitude is held by a minority and is not generally respected in a world ruled by knowledge. To most people, beliefs are paramount in life. Religious beliefs have great importance, particularly in our society. Thus the nation's Constitution established full protection to individuals and religious organizations for practicing their faith; as a matter of fact, they enjoy certain privileges and freedoms not granted to secular organizations.

The Use of Drugs for Spiritual Experiences

In general, religious people and those who are dedicated to serving humanity have not used drugs for the purpose of reaching spiritual goals. However, as a result of hallucinogenic drug research, LSD and other compounds have been used for some religious experiences, spiritual development, expansion of the mind or consciousness, and achievement of enlightenment. Many have reported experiencing states similar to those found in the literature of saints, enlightened masters, and mystics.

Frequently individuals experimenting with hallucinogenic drugs describe their experiences in some of the following ways: "A trip into heaven," "I was in the presence of God," "I saw Jesus in front of me," "The incredible feeling of oneness was overwhelming," "It was like going to hell and back," or "I saw monsters and demons." These drugs evoke visions in people today just as the plants and fungi did centuries ago.

People continue to be caught in the circles of humanity's conditioning, unaware of their cyclic behavior. The vision-eliciting plants once used exclusively by the medicine man are now used by the populace.

This circular behavior is depicted in the following diagram.

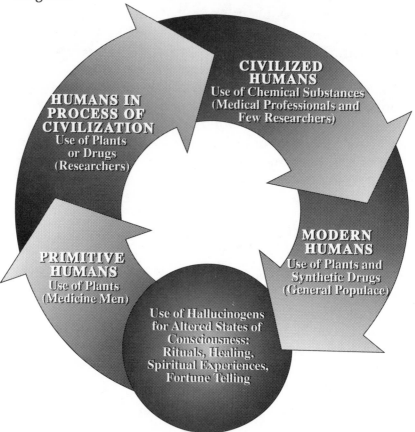

Despite knowledge, progress, and civilization, we have not changed as much as we think!

Through medical research we have changed the chemical structure of some derivatives of plants or have produced new synthetic drugs; the purpose of their use, however, remains essentially the same. Perhaps an added reason for modern men and women to consume these mind-expanding drugs, as well as alcohol, cocaine, and similar drugs, is as a kind of entertainment, an escape from the consequences of our way of living, with its tensions and fears.

Traditional Religious Experiences

Throughout civilization, individual experiences, visions, premonitions, and anthropomorphic images have proliferated into a variety of beliefs and organized religions.

Altered states of consciousness are considered signs of the Unmanifest, the unknown, or God. These states may be experienced with or without drugs or other external stimuli. Fasting, meditation, and deep hypnotic trances are known to produce the same effect. In addition to these, there are natural experiences, not elicited by any artificial means, which do not seem to differ in impact or in lasting results in the life of the experiencer. These are the religious or spiritual experiences occurring within many seekers of truth and believers in the divine.

For centuries people have meditated, practiced various spiritual techniques and rituals, sacrificed, and even mutilated their bodies in order to go beyond the carnal experience of themselves. What power or energy could be strong enough to lead to abuses of the flesh and killing for the purpose of reaching God or converting others to a belief? Such human activity is not yet thoroughly understood. Explanations are attempted through psychological and philosophical theories or religious rationalization based on the same conditioned consciousness that produces this type of behavior in the first place. These kinds of actions and their subsequent explanations have a merry-go-round effect. Nothing is altered, though it is said we understand.

In a sect connected with Islam, the Shia's, believers inflict cuts on their own heads or on those of others in honor of the martyrs of their religion. They then parade in the streets in a bloody, fanatical frenzy. In their minds there are good reasons and justifications for this behavior.

All the explanations in the world have not contributed to a radical change in the destructive tendencies of humanity or in the beliefs that justify them. Nor has there been any substantial degree of self-investigation or introspection. On the contrary, most people are satisfied with the explanations and continue to exist in a somnolent consciousness.

While abusive practices are still in existence, there are others, such as some Buddhist sects and Zen, that have as powerful an effect but are not as violent. Cultivated through thousands of years, Buddhism is based on the enlightenment experience and teachings of its founder and is peaceful in nature. Nonetheless, occasional acts of violence such as cutting a sexual member in order to obtain nirvana or reach the Unmanifest, have been known to occur in these religious practices. By and large, however, the widely sought experience of enlightenment is a quiet, peaceful, and nonsacrificial pursuit.

Currently, Christianity advocates self-sacrifice without violence, for the sake of rewards in this life (finding God or Jesus) or the next (going to heaven). Mother Teresa, an example of a self-sacrificing believer, is respected all over the world for her love and total dedication to the alleviation of suffering in humanity.

Some spiritual practices such as Zen and Taoism have developed without a major emphasis on sacrifice of the body. The main pursuit for most of the aspirants is enlightenment, focusing on selflessness and simplicity. There is an emphasis on nature, wisdom, and the achievement of harmony with the universe.

These are generalities and are not meant to reduce these philosophies simply to the description presented here. The point is that the unknown is sought in these philosophies, just as it is in the others mentioned. We remain fascinated and preoccupied with the Unmanifest and keep trying to understand it, obtain it, explain it, as well as teach and practice it, through belief.

Nontraditional Spirituality

The New Age spirituality, while basing its pursuits on the old belief in oneness, Christ-consciousness, God-consciousness, and so on, actually has a new orientation: the attainment of happiness, abundance, and full self-expression. There is nothing wrong with self-expression or the attainment of happiness or abundance. It is only the consequences in general that are of concern. When a great majority behaves selfishly, with disregard for others, then any of these three pursuits—self-expression, happiness, or riches—may be detrimental. For example, the accumulation of wealth and property by a few in a society may take away from others. Doing in excess what brings pleasure— such as drinking, smoking, not working for a living and thus depending on others—adds to the societal burden. Smoking in public places without regard for the health of others causes cancer and lung damage and heart disease in non smokers. The artistic expression through powerful loudspeakers of modern rock musicians causes damage to the delicate structure of the ears.

When self-expression is spontaneous and loving in nature, however, it contributes to the well-being of the whole. When abundance is shared with those who are deprived, it is a blessing. The drive toward attainment of happiness, abundance, and full self-expression is promoted in religions such as Science of Mind, Christian TV evangelism ("God wants you to be prosperous") and in spiritual practices, channeling, and psychic-healing circles.

Quite often this new trend in thinking, instead of separating the carnal from the spiritual or being self-sacrificing, is actually self-serving. Belief in oneness ("we are the world") is only a pseudo-oneness focusing on the "me," for the *belief* in full self-expression emphasizes individualism; thus separativeness remains. However, there are some sincere leaders, such as Ram Dass, who became prominent in the New Age movement and who are now advocating selfless *true service*. A pitfall for followers is that serving others may be used as a self-satisfying activity, thus still serving the "me." True service comes from the heart; it is all-giving without need for reward.

Many people, who may or may not consider themselves religious or part of the New Age movement, do not follow a self-centered type of belief. They are sincere, true searchers of truth who are willing to confront the reality of the human predicament within themselves. They are responsible beings doing, with great integrity, all they can to be aware themselves and bring about awareness in the world without separating themselves as special individuals. These are people from all walks of life, religious people and nonbelievers alike, lovingly helping to heal others, sharing harmoniously their life of dedication in the service of humanity. Some feel blessed with mystical experiences of God, yet others live a life of service without adherence to a religious practice or a traditional belief.

Spirituality Today: Is It Conditioning?

The concept of God has taken a different orientation for many members of the most popular religions. It has changed, for some people, from an anthropomorphic God to a God who is everything and everyone. Reports of spiritual experiences within the laity validate this view of God, and it is now being adopted by many Catholics and other Christian worshippers. The belief that God is one has given rise to the conviction that "I am God" or "I Am," propagated by Joel Goldsmith, a Westerner, and by several Indian gurus such as Sai Baba, Sri Nisargaddta Maharaj, and others.

A literal interpretation of this concept is an inevitable consequence of the divisive consciousness of humankind. While intellectually accepting the belief that "you and I are one," people actually behave in separateness; they treat families, friends, and fellow workers with the same irreverence that has persisted in humanity as a whole. Respect or reverence remains within the confines of the church, temple, or meditation hall. If we truly saw God in ourselves as well as in others, we would constantly behave with appropriate deep respect and love. Although both traditional and contemporary religions stress this concept above all, millions of followers are not *living* it in their daily relationships.

The belief that *I am God* may be a trap. To the conditioned mind trained to believe in good and evil, God represents only goodness. Thus, thinking of oneself as God inevitably excludes evil from self. Unaware, the person will project evil on others while claiming oneness. Nothing has changed; separatism remains, basically as a result of divisionary thinking. That is one of the main points of this book.

Regardless of how we interpret (or trap ourselves with) our own psychic experiences, we have to recognize the powerful impact these experiences have on the individual. Many people have reported a total turnaround in their lives after certain psychic or spiritual events. The depth of feeling is such that it has made believers out of skeptics. Churches are full of worshippers testifying to the power of the Holy Spirit, God, or Jesus; meditators report having achieved altered states of consciousness, nirvana, levitation, peak experiences, and enlightenment. During all of these experiences, there is an indescribable feeling of oneness and love, which may be fleeting, temporary, or lasting.

Why do psychic phenomena continue to manifest in the minds of human beings associated with superior power, goodness, love, and in a series of images and visions? Is there something basic that is beyond this conditioning? Is there a basic goodness? Or are all the experiences one assigns to the Unmanifest, God, the unknown, or Buddha-nature still products of the conditioned mind? What are the images that appear in waking consciousness as well as in dreams and meditations? What are the overwhelming feelings of love that cause certain people to dedicate their entire lives to serving humanity? What is the source of visions experienced under the influence of hallucinogenic plants and drugs, and why are they similar to the visions of the mystics?

Are all of these mere chemical changes that evoke memories of the collective unconscious postulated by Carl Jung? And why does the vision of Buddha not appear to a Christian or the vision of Jesus to a Buddhist?

All of us must answer these questions for ourselves without relying on anyone else's theoretical explanations or beliefs. It is necessary for each of us to examine our own cultural, religious, and societal background; to explore the images associated with the psychic phenomena we experience and their behavioral consequences. Furthermore, we need to explore our own mind structure truthfully, openly, without reservations; observe objectively our own natural expression of spirituality (love, goodness, images) outside any frame of reference and *without beliefs*. Otherwise, we continue to be in awe of the experiences themselves, with no awareness of the historical truth of humanity's interpretations and the consequent behavior.

It is perplexing to observe a humanity whose members repeatedly profess and experience love and oneness, while they remain trapped in primitive emotional structures of fear and territorialism that result in religious wars.

In spite of countless experiences of love and oneness, men and women have yet to transform themselves. They have yet to discover that they are, like the caterpillar, responsible for preparing for their own inevitable process of transformation; therefore they remain asleep. Idolatry of images supersedes the living expression of love, and the fleeting moments of psychic experience remain only in memory as beautiful, powerful phenomenological events.

🌹 *Whatever is expressed in humanity as a whole is manifested in each one of us as an individual, for each of us represents, as it were, a hologram of mankind. Thus each of us is responsible for the whole.*

Psychic Phenomena: Energy Fields

Thousands of years of recorded psychic phenomena point to the existence of a reality beyond the present, limited consciousness of human beings. Indeed, when one is relaxed, quiet, the mind emptied of ambitions and self-centeredness, the overwhelming experience of love is manifested. This love has no conditions, no opposites. A mind preoccupied with survival and fear cannot be open to a transcendental experience that brings about a total shift in the whole organism. *We are responsible for emptying our own crowded minds.*

We may not be able to prove scientifically that paranormal experiences have an objective reality (as our linear minds perceive reality). Still, we cannot deny the existence of something beyond our own thinking process. It would be more accurate to say that we have *no-thing* experiences, because we cannot feel or touch the images of our visions. Normally others cannot share them with us at the same moment, as they can share a sunset or a work of art. However, some experiences of love, as well as ESP, may be experienced simultaneously with others and point to a different kind of connection between human beings.

There is a belief, particularly in the New Age movement, that if enough individuals experience peace or love, it will create an energy field that will have an impact on the whole of humanity. In this theory, consciousness expands from an individual who has become aware to others at large; when many individuals are in that new awareness, it creates an energy field that expands to include others in the world.

The now famous *hundredth monkey theory* supports this. This theory was formulated when a group of scientists observing monkeys on a South Seas island saw a female monkey wash a potato for the first time. Other monkeys predictably mimicked her behavior. However, after a *critical mass* (about a hundred monkeys washing potatoes) was reached, the same behavior appeared unexpectedly in a group of monkeys living on another island without any contact with the original group that displayed the behavior. It has since been explained that communication occurred by means of an energy field connecting the monkeys. This is a simplification of the morphogenetic field theory; the reader may wish to refer to Rupert Sheldrake's book, *A New Science of Life* (Los Angeles: J.P. Tarcher, 1981) for a more detailed discussion of energy fields.

This occurrence among monkeys may be considered miraculous, because its mechanism is still unknown. Do monkeys have ESP? Is what we call ESP actually an energy field? Perhaps humanity is constantly communicating through extrasensory perception without being aware of it. If so, it would explain some remarkable historical occurrences. For example, the Egyptians and the Mayans both constructed pyramids even though there was apparently no physical contact between the two civilizations.

Several other theories have been formulated to explain this phenomenon, but the energy-field theory is beginning to gain acceptance.

Taking into consideration the possibility of the existence of energy fields, can we ask ourselves if in our daily living we experience this kind of connection to the rest of humanity? Can we realize *being* the energy field? Are we in constant communication and unaware of it? Is this the unmanifested oneness? Unmanifested in the sense that we cannot perceive it through our sensorial functioning. What prevents most of humanity from experiencing this kind of reality? It is up to each of us to find out.

Life

Existing in a mostly "unconscious" consciousness, human beings have not been able to truly "live" life.

This statement may be confusing to some, but through a deeper look into humanity's conditioning, unawareness, and limitations of the daily thinking process, this *unconsciousness* will be revealed, and *living life* will become evident through awareness of our present somnolent consciousness.

We are mostly unconscious of the universe, even though this is where we exist. We largely know only the stars and planets we can see with the naked eye. Only in recent times have we been able to perceive more distant celestial bodies through the technology of large telescopes and satellite probes. However even these sophisticated tools have a limited capacity.

In our daily thinking we normally do not include the earth or the universe. We are limited to more immediate areas that satisfy our survival needs. Thus, our consciousness is limited within the walls of conditioning and acculturation, as well as emotional and physical needs. As someone has said, we do not take time to smell the flowers. We definitely do not take into consideration the rest of humanity. We hoard while others starve; we pollute the environment and strip the earth of its resources with our industries. A mind busy with survival and gratification has very little space to experience the Unmanifest.

Persons living in areas where robbery, gang violence, drug abuse, and assault are rife, feel threatened; fear permeates their waking consciousness. On a global scale, humanity's mind is preoccupied with national boundaries for survival, thus conflict is inevitable. The experiences of love and visions of goodness become part of a system of beliefs designed to protect those boundaries.

We begin to think that life is only about the circumstances we are in, the emotions we feel, or the pleasures we seek. When we lose our job or our money, we feel that life is terrible. A striking example of this is the many suicides that occurred during the stock market crash of 1929. Life was so unbearable to those human beings that they were driven to end it. When circumstances are to our liking or feel pleasurable, then life is wonderful. Being "in love" is a classic example. And so we believe that life is either good or bad, and we suffer! As soon as we lose something or someone we are attached to, we feel part of our life is gone. When we acquire or satisfy our pleasures and needs, we feel alive.

This is living the circumstance, not living life; it is only feeling our inner reactions to the activities of our external world to which we have attributed the importance of life itself.

Circumstances are the consequence of the way we live, what we have conceived through our knowledge. They are tantamount to culture, to conditioning, to civilization.

Life is water and earth; a seed, a sprout, a flower, a tree; fish, animals, human beings. Life is the moon, the sun, all stars, planets, and other celestial bodies. Life is space! To experience the all-encompassing space is to live life.

Living life means being open to all possibilities, being vulnerable to the unknown and free to experience that which is as yet unmanifested to our senses.

When we *live life* we do not anthropomorphize, thus we do not venerate the memory of our visions or images of altered states of consciousness. We do not engage in rituals to appease nature or gods, nor do we attribute our actions to angels or devils as an excuse for killing in the name of religion, nationalism, or territorialism. We do not build houses of worship or statues. We do not have preachers, gurus, or teachers. We do not revere knowledge. We do not judge or evaluate one another.

When we *live life* we cooperate rather than compete; we neither hoard nor starve.

When we *live life* we are in oneness, beyond all opposites. Life is neither great nor terrible.

When we *live life* we are in aware consciousness, not *somnolent* consciousness.

When we *live life* we exist in the Unmanifest, the *ultimate reality of space* that is the universe, the stars and planets; human beings, animals, and fish; the trees, flowers, sprouts, and seeds; the water and the earth.

Space is energy, quiescent life. Space is the Unmanifest— the Unmanifest, which is eternal love.

AFTERWORD

You and I have come through an arduous process of interrogation. It must have seemed to you at times repetitive, perhaps boring or perturbing.

The brain, remembering what it has read (in my case what it wrote) says, "Well, I already knew that," or "You said that before," or "Why don't you teach me something new!"

I'm afraid, my friend, that I had nothing new to teach. I respected your intelligence and knowledge by offering only questions and suggestions for you to examine, nothing more.

Perhaps your greatest task has just begun. It is in the process of life itself that you are going to experience the fruition of all we have explored. It is in your daily relationships that you are going to observe the other as yourself. Or perhaps you are one of the many people who, having experienced teachers such as David Bohm or Krishnamurti, have already begun inquiry. If you have read this book completely and looked anew without comparisons, you have *lived* the kind of exploration that Krishnamurti beseeched his listeners and readers to experience.

You cannot go through a process of sincere investigation and not be deeply affected. This book might not have been more than a seed in the garden of your mind. Of course, I would like to think that it has been more like a needed nutrient for your already existing process of flowering; the seed itself is actually you, your being.

In a recent meeting with my friends, one person was trying to describe my work and she said, "Ligia, you are a catalyst." My image at the time was that of an enzyme, a kind of protein substance that accelerates physical processes. If this book that has come across your path can be like an enzyme, a facilitator that assists in your own process, then we have together contributed, to the best of our abilities, to humanity as a whole. Our conduct in life will be the reflection of our contribution.

It is clear to me that it is possible for human beings to live with all the knowledge, the material things, and to reap all the benefits of this civilization designed by our own intelligence without suffering or endangering the planet.

A mature, responsible way of living comes about when we live harmoniously—that is, within our own integrity. By integrity I mean wholeness, not lacking any of the elements to function as a unit. Thus when we act with this kind of integrity we, my friends, are in a consciousness of wholeness. To me, this is being "holyness," a spiritual state in which the physical body is not separate. Thus, life is a holy state of love.

When you experience love and compassion, humanity is experiencing the same. You and I and humanity, though separate in appearance, are a whole movement of energy on the planet. All together we are the movement of the energy of the universe.

My friend, thank you for being.

Ligia

About Self-Studies Foundation

Self-Studies Foundation was founded by Ligia Dantes in 1974 as the Self-Studies Institute in San Francisco. When she moved to Ojai in 1984 she changed it to Self-Studies Foundation, a non-profit, tax-exempt organization.

The purpose of Self-Studies is to provide a special space for individuals to share in the process of self-discovery. It is a place to address honestly, simply and directly the serious issues of life and to open oneself to true insight which is not just more conceptualizing. A unique vitality is created when thoughtful and responsible persons gather to inquire deeply in an atmosphere of love and caring.

Self-Studies does not advocate the use of any spiritual practices or teachings resting solely on the authority of one individual. It does not engage in philosophical debates, psychotherapy, or esoteric practices. The instruments which have been found to be most useful to individuals serious about self-discovery are dialogue, meditation and retreats. These functions permit the individual to move into a state of relaxation and silence where insight may occur. The primary focus of this organization is to provide a peaceful physical environment and atmosphere of love and caring for these activities to take place.

For more information write: **Self-Studies Foundation**
P.O. Box 93
Ojai, CA 93023